CHEMISTRY HOMEWORK

MATTHEW BOULTON CAMPUS

Sayira Shaheen

for OC ... TE AWARDS

Gareth Pritchard and Ann Tiernan

Series editor: Bob McDuell

Heinemann Educational Publishers,
Halley Court, Jordan Hill, Oxford, OX2 8EJ
A division of Reed Educational & Professional Publishing Ltd
Heinemann is a registered trademark of Reed Educational & Professional Publishing Limited

OXFORD MELBOURNE AUCKLAND
JOHANNESBURG BLANTYRE GABORONE
IBADAN PORTSMOUTH NH (USA) CHICAGO

First published 2001

ISBN 0 435 58280 1

05 04 03 02 01
10 9 8 7 6 5 4 3 2 1

Edited by Helen Roberts

Index by Indexing Specialists

Typeset and illustrated by 🏹 Tek-Art, Croydon, Surrey

Printed and bound in Great Britain by Scotprint, East Lothian

Acknowledgements

P5 Q1, artwork Hodder and Stoughton Education Limited; Q3, artwork © John Holman 1996, *Material World*, Nelson Thornes. P12 Q1 artwork Hodder and Stoughton. P24 Q3 artwork © John Holman 1996, *Material World*, Nelson Thornes. P36 Q4 and Q5 artwork Basil Blackwell. P47 Q2 and P60 Q3 artwork © Andrew Hunt and Alan Sykes, reprinted by permission of Pearson Education Limited.

The publishers have made every effort to trace the copyright holders, but if they have inadvertently overlooked any, they will be pleased to make the necessary arrangements at the first opportunity.

Introduction

This book provides homework for students taking chemistry as part of OCR specification A double-award science or OCR specification A separate-award Chemistry. It accompanies the student course books for OCR A double-award and separate-award chemistry (ISBNs 0 435 58293 3 and 0 435 58292 5, respectively).

There is one page of homework for each double-page spread in the student book. This makes it easy to see which homework may be set following lessons based on a particular double-page spread.

Where students can take the course book home, this homework book will supply the extra work to be done at home. Where the course book is not available, the homework book provides:

• a list of key points for each spread
• important diagrams for reference
• the full and detailed glossary from the separate-award chemistry course book
• key data for reference.

Students should use these data sheets and Periodic Table to find atomic numbers and relative atomic masses.

The answers to all of the questions in the homework book are available on the CD-ROM. They can be used to mark the work or printed out and given to students for self-marking.

The questions in the homework book can be used in lessons where the teacher is absent. Students can work through the relevant double page spread in the course book and then attempt questions from the homework book. They could then be given the answers from the CD-ROM towards the end of the lesson.

The homework book allows differentiated homework if required. The questions in the homework book are set at three levels:

■ standard demand – aimed at C–D grades
◆ standard/high demand – aimed at A–B grades
◇ high demand – aimed at A* grade.

Material marked with an **H** is for higher tier only.

IDEAS AND EVIDENCE questions focus on how science is evaluated and presented, and the power and limitations of science in addressing industrial, social and environmental issues.

For students needing further help there is additional material on the CD-ROM which can be modified to suit the individual needs of students. This could be put together as a booklet for each Teaching block, perhaps incorporating KS3 Summary sheets and modified Student checklists where statements in bold (higher tier only) are removed.

We hope that this Homework book will help students to be successful.

Contents

Teaching block **A1**

Water

Teaching block **A2**

Acids, bases and salts

Teaching block **A3**

Metals and redox reactions

Teaching block **A4**

Carbon chemistry

Teaching block **A5**

Quantitative chemistry

Teaching block **A6**

Electrochemistry and its applications

1.1 Hazards and safety

Key points

- A study of chemistry involves using chemicals.
- We are fortunate that we now know much more about the hazards associated with these substances.

- Chemists use a warning system to advise of possible dangers.
- The system uses signs known as the Hazchem code.

1 The picture shows some students in a chemistry laboratory.

Find six hazards in the picture.

Explain why each one is dangerous.

2 At petrol pumps in garages, there are notices which state:

> *Extinguish all naked lights.*

Explain why these notices are put up.

3 A manufacturer has brought out an effective weed-killer powder 'Weedgo'. It is poisonous if eaten and causes irritation when in contact with the skin or eyes. Design a poster which warns gardeners about any precautions they should take when using 'Weedgo'.

4 Ask an adult to help you check at home for five containers which have Hazchem symbols on them. Make a table like the one given, showing:

a the names of the substances you have found

b the Hazchem symbol on each

c the reason the symbol is present.

substance	symbol	reason

5 Sue is a laboratory technician. She has to make some dilute sulphuric acid from concentrated sulphuric acid and water. She knows that a lot of heat energy is given out when these two substances are mixed together.

Suggest why Sue adds the sulphuric acid slowly to water with continuous stirring, rather than adding water to the sulphuric acid.

6 Sodium and potassium are highly reactive metals. They readily combine with oxygen to form a metal oxide, e.g. Na_2O, and with water to form hydrogen and a metal hydroxide, e.g. KOH.

a Explain why these metals are stored under oil in tightly capped bottles.

b Write an equation for the reaction of:

  i sodium burning in oxygen

  ii potassium reacting with water.

c When potassium is added to water, it melts, catches fire and darts around the surface of the water. The last little bit might even explode.

If a teacher wants to show this reaction to a class, suggest what precautions must be taken to make the experiment as safe as possible.

7 A science class are discussing the ways in which a chip-pan fire can be extinguished.

a Anne suggests that the burning pan should be carried to the door and taken outside.

b Ben suggests pouring water on the flames.

c Cath suggests covering the pan with a damp cloth.

Discuss the merits and dangers of each of these three methods and decide which is the safest method to use.

1.2 Compounds

Key points

- Compounds contain two or more types of atom chemically combined.
- The particles in compounds are held together by strong bonds.

- Chemical formulae are used to represent compounds.
- Compounds have properties which are different from those of the elements from which they are made.

1 Here are the formulae of some compounds. For each formula, write down the symbols present and the elements they represent. The first one has been done as an example.

NaCl   Na, sodium and Cl, chlorine

a CuO	b $ZnCO_3$	c $Ca(OH)_2$
d CO_2	e ZnS	f $ZnSO_4$
g NH_4Br	h KNO_3	i $CaCl_2$

2 When two elements combine together, the name of the second element changes to 'ide', e.g. NaCl is sodium chloride.

If there are **two** atoms of oxygen or sulphur as the second element, the name becomes 'dioxide' or 'disulphide'.

If there is an OH is in the formula, it is a hydroxide.

Use this information to name the following compounds.

a FeO	b CO_2	c CaS	d Na_2O
e PbI_2	f KOH	g $MgCl_2$	h $AlCl_3$
i LiOH	j SO_2	k K_2S	l $Ca(OH)_2$
m KF	n $Al(OH)_3$		

3 The names of compounds containing certain groups of elements in which oxygen appears end in 'ate'. For example:

SO_4 is a sulphate
CO_3 is a carbonate
NO_3 is a nitrate
PO_4 is a phosphate.

Name the following compounds.

a Na_2SO_4	b $CaCO_3$	c KNO_3	d $AlPO_4$
e $MgCO_3$	f $BaSO_4$	g Li_3PO_4	h $AgNO_3$

4 The table shows the combining power of some elements and groups.

The combining power is connected with the number of electrons the elements use in making bonds. Certain elements can have more than one combining power if the number of electrons they use in making bonds can change.

combining power			
I (one)	**II** (two)	**III** (three)	**IV** (four)
Li Na K Ag F Cl Br I	Mg Ca Ba Cu Fe Zn Pb O S	Al Fe	Pb
OH NO_3	CO_3 SO_4	PO_4	

When substances are made, the combining power must be used up.

So calcium (combining power of 2) will need two atoms of fluorine (combining power of 1) to make calcium fluoride, CaF_2.

Use the table to help you write formulae for the following substances.

a sodium nitrate
b silver iodide
c calcium bromide
d lithium sulphate
e copper(II) hydroxide
f barium carbonate
g iron(II) chloride
h iron(III) oxide
i lead(IV) iodide
j lead(II) sulphate
k aluminium hydroxide
l zinc carbonate
m magnesium fluoride
n iron(III) sulphide
o lead(II) nitrate
p sodium phosphate

1.3 Equations

Key points

- Chemical reactions can be represented by word equations that show all the reactants and products.
- It is more useful to represent chemical reactions using symbols.
- Symbol equations may need to be balanced.
- Chemical reactions that involve charged particles, called ions, can be represented by ionic equations.

1 Write word equations for the reaction between the following elements:

a hydrogen and chlorine

b sodium and fluorine

c magnesium and oxygen

d carbon and plentiful oxygen

e carbon and limited oxygen

f hydrogen and oxygen.

2 Here are three general reactions.

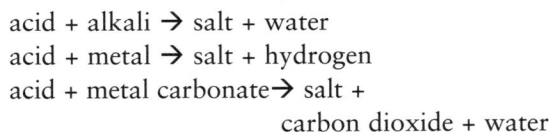

acid + alkali → salt + water

acid + metal → salt + hydrogen

acid + metal carbonate→ salt + carbon dioxide + water

Complete these word equations:

a sodium hydroxide + hydrochloric acid

b sodium carbonate + sulphuric acid

c magnesium + hydrochloric acid

d calcium hydroxide + nitric acid

e potassium carbonate + sulphuric acid.

3 Write balanced equations for these word equations:

a potassium carbonate + hydrochloric acid →
potassium chloride + carbon dioxide + water

b sodium hydroxide + sulphuric acid →
sodium sulphate + water

c zinc + sulphuric acid → zinc sulphate + hydrogen

d sodium carbonate+ nitric acid →
sodium nitrate + carbon dioxide + water.

4 When a metal (M^H)higher in the reactivity series is added to a solution of a salt of a metal (M^L) lower in that series, a displacement reaction takes place. The general equation is:

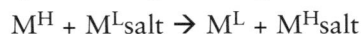

$$M^H + M^L salt → M^L + M^H salt$$

Write balanced equations for the following reactions:

a magnesium + copper(II) sulphate

b zinc + silver nitrate

c calcium + lead(II) nitrate

d iron + copper(II) chloride

e aluminium + zinc sulphate.

5 Balance the following equations:

a $KOH + H_2SO_4 → K_2SO_4 + H_2O$

b $CuO + HCl → CuCl_2 + H_2O$

c $NaHCO_3 → Na_2CO_3 + H_2O + CO_2$

d $Zn(NO_3)_2 → PbO + NO_2 + O_2$

e $C_2H_4 + O_2 → CO_2 + H_2O$

f $CuO + NH_3 → N_2 + Cu + H_2O$

g $CO + Fe_2O_3 → CO_2 + Fe$

6 When converting a balanced equation into an ionic equation, you can assume that all acids, bases, alkalis and solutions of salts become ions. Water and elements that are normally gases remain as molecules.

Here is an example.

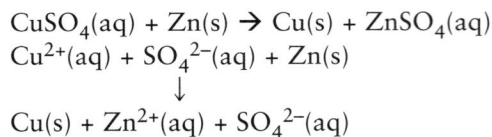

$$CuSO_4(aq) + Zn(s) → Cu(s) + ZnSO_4(aq)$$
$$Cu^{2+}(aq) + SO_4^{2-}(aq) + Zn(s)$$
$$\downarrow$$
$$Cu(s) + Zn^{2+}(aq) + SO_4^{2-}(aq)$$

The 'spectator ions' ($SO_4^{2-}(aq)$)can be missed out, so the ionic equation becomes:

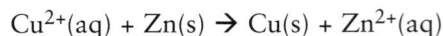

$$Cu^{2+}(aq) + Zn(s) → Cu(s) + Zn^{2+}(aq)$$

Rewrite the following equations as ionic equations.

a $Mg(s) + ZnCl_2(aq) → MgCl_2(aq) + Zn(s)$

b $NH_4Cl(aq) + NaOH(aq) → NaCl(aq) + NH_3(g) + H_2O(l)$

c $Fe(s) + 2HCl(aq) → FeCl_2(aq) + H_2(g)$

d $Cl_2(g) + 2FeCl_2(aq) → 2FeCl_3(aq)$

e $K_2CO_3(aq) + 2HCl(aq) → 2KCl(aq) + CO_2(g) + H_2O(l)$

f $CuSO_4(aq) + 2NaOH(aq) → Na_2SO_4(aq) + Cu(OH)_2(s)$

1.4 Limestone

Key points

- Limestone is a plentiful and useful mineral.
- It contains mostly calcium carbonate.
- It is used to manufacture glass and cement.

- It decomposes to quicklime (calcium oxide) and carbon dioxide when strongly heated.
- Quicklime and slaked lime are used to neutralise excess acidity in lakes and on the land.

1 Limestone can be converted into quicklime (calcium oxide) in a lime kiln (see the diagram below).

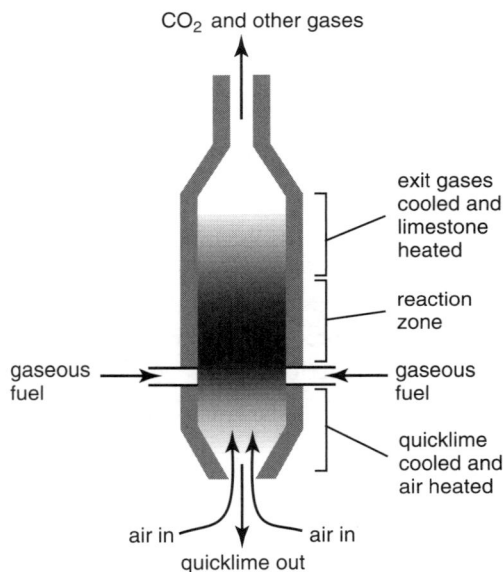

CO$_2$ and other gases

exit gases cooled and limestone heated

reaction zone

gaseous fuel — — gaseous fuel

quicklime cooled and air heated

air in — quicklime out — air in

a The working temperature of about 1200 °C is reached by burning a gaseous fuel. Give **two** reasons why air is pushed in at the base of the kiln.

b Write a word equation to show what happens to the limestone inside the kiln.

c If the gaseous fuel is methane ('natural gas') and the air supply is plentiful, write a word equation for what happens to the methane inside the kiln.

2 Complete these sentences choosing words **only** from the list.

**exothermic   endothermic   limestone   quicklime
slaked lime   water**

Calcium oxide, also known as _____, is easily converted into calcium hydroxide, also known as _____ , by adding _____ to it. The reaction gives out much heat, turning some of the _____ into steam. It is therefore an example of an _____ reaction.

IDEAS AND EVIDENCE

3 What environmental problems are present when large-scale quarrying of limestone takes place?

4 Here is some data about the process and costs involved when limestone is converted into quicklime in a limekiln which uses fuel gas to provide the energy.

Capacity of kiln = 50 tonnes of limestone
Number of employees needed = 5
Time taken to convert 50 tonnes of limestone into quicklime = 4 hours
Cost of limestone = £5 per tonne
Cost of energy = £4 per minute
Cost of wages = £10 per hour per person
Cost of maintenance = £1 per minute.

a Work out the costs for a manufacturer to buy in 50 tonnes of limestone and convert it all into quicklime.

b The firm's marketing manager decides that the process needs to make a profit of about £6 per tonne of quicklime.

Assume that the process makes 25 tonnes of saleable quicklime from 50 tonnes of limestone.

Decide which of the following selling prices per tonne of quicklime would be a sensible one to choose.

£30   £70   £100

1.5 Acids

Key points

- Acids have characteristic reactions with carbonates, alkalis and some metals.
- These characteristic reactions enable predictions to be made about the reactions of acids that may be unfamiliar.

- Acids can be present in rain and this can cause damage to building materials such as metals and carbonate rocks.
- Bases and alkalis can be used to neutralise acids. This can be on a small laboratory scale or on a larger scale, e.g. in lakes affected by acid rain.

1

Gardeners test the pH of soil to find out which plants will grow. They shake a sample of the soil with water and test the pH of the water using universal indicator solution. It is easier to see the colour of the indicator if the soil is removed from the water.

a   How can soil be removed from water?

b   Design a garden soil pH test kit for gardeners. What equipment will you put in your kit?

c   Design a leaflet to show gardeners how to use your kit. Include diagrams and step by step instructions.

d   What advice would you give to gardeners who find that their soil is too acidic?

e   Small, electronic pH meters are also sold in garden centres. What advantages do these have over ordinary test kits?

2   This is a list of salts. Each one can be made by neutralising an acid. Which acid is each made from?

a   ammonium nitrate (used as a fertiliser)

b   sodium chloride (common salt)

c   iron sulphate (used in 'iron tablets')

3   Sulphuric acid dissolves rust, Fe_2O_3, from iron sheets. Car body parts are dipped in sulphuric acid before they are painted. This is the (unbalanced) equation for the reaction.

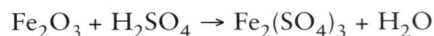

$$Fe_2O_3 + H_2SO_4 \rightarrow Fe_2(SO_4)_3 + H_2O$$

a   Copy and balance the equation.

b   Explain why the iron is only left in the acid for a few seconds.

4   Sulphuric acid is used during the making of cleaning products including shower gel and kitchen cleaners. Many of these products have sodium hydroxide added to them to remove left over traces of sulphuric acid.

a   Write a word and symbol equation for the reaction between sodium hydroxide and sulphuric acid.

b   Why is it important to remove sulphuric acid from household products?

c   What type of reaction happens between the sulphuric acid and the sodium hydroxide?

d   Look at the labels on cosmetics and household cleaners. Make a list of three products that contain sodium hydroxide. How many of these also contain compounds of sulphates? Where do you think the sulphates came from?

1.6 Hydrogen

Key points

- Hydrogen, H_2, is a colourless gas.
- A mixture of hydrogen and air explodes when a burning splint is put near it.
- The combustion of hydrogen produes water as the only product.

- The combination of an element, such as hydrogen, with oxygen is am example of an oxidation reaction.
- The opposite of oxidation is called reduction. It is the removal of oxygen from a compound.
- The reaction between hydrogen and oxygen can be made to produce useful energy.

1 Some students make fact cards to help them revise for tests. Here is the start of a fact card about hydrogen.

> **Hydrogen**
>
> H_2 is a colourless gas with no smell.
> H_2 is the lightest gas, about 20 times lighter than air.
> The test for H_2 is ...

a Copy the fact card. Use your classwork notes to add other important facts about hydrogen.

b Suppose you were asked to talk about the chemistry of hydrogen to younger pupils. Choose two facts about hydrogen. Draw cartoons to illustrate these facts to younger pupils.

2 An aeroplane has been converted to use liquid hydrogen as a fuel.

a What advantages does hydrogen have for use as an aeroplane fuel?

b If the fuel tank was damaged in a plane crash, the hydrogen would be less likely to cause an explosion than leaking petrol. Explain why.

3 This equation shows how copper oxide reacts with hydrogen to make copper.

$$CuO + H_2 \rightarrow Cu + \ldots\ldots$$

a What is the name of the other compound made in the reaction?

b Kim wrote these notes in her exercise book about the reaction.

> This is an example of an <u>exothermic</u> reaction. Copper has been <u>reduced</u> and hydrogen has been <u>oxidised</u>.

Use the glossary to help you to explain what the underlined words mean.

4 In 1937 the Hindenburg balloon ship exploded killing 36 people. It was filled with hydrogen. In 1986, seven astronauts died in the Challenger space shuttle when hydrogen fuel exploded after being mixed with oxygen.

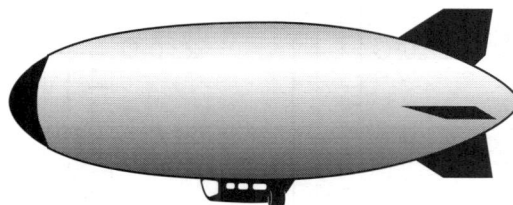

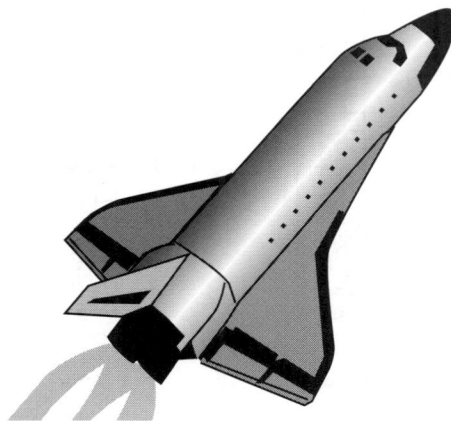

a Imagine you were responsible for safety on a balloon ship like the Hindenburg. What safety advice would you give to the passengers and crew?

b Helium is now used to fill passenger balloons. Find helium in the Periodic Table. Suggest reasons why helium is a good choice for filling these balloons.

c Why does the space shuttle carry tanks of oxygen in addition to tanks of hydrogen?

d What are the advantages of using tanks of oxygen rather than tanks of air?

1.7 Energy transfer (1)

1 The thermometer diagrams show the temperatures of some hydrochloric acid before a piece of magnesium is added to it and immediately after the reaction is complete.

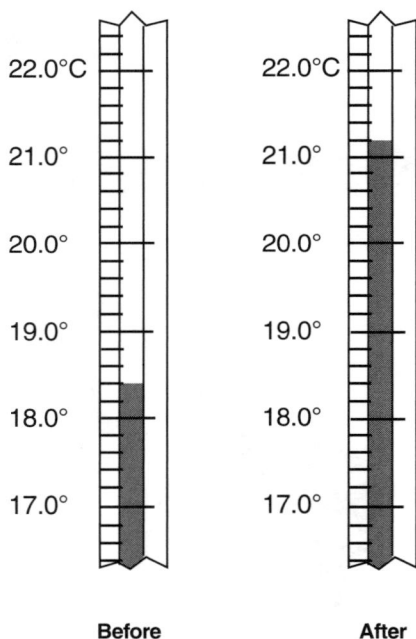

Before   **After**

a Work out the difference in the temperatures shown on the thermometers.

b Decide from these temperatures whether the reaction is exothermic or endothermic and give your reason.

c Write a word equation for the reaction which takes place between the magnesium and the hydrochloric acid.

2 Sue adds some ammonium carbonate to a test-tube containing some water. She holds the test-tube in her hand and realises that as the ammonium carbonate dissolves, the test-tube starts to feel much colder. Explain what is happening.

3 Tom puts a thermometer into some water in a test-tube and notes the temperature. He adds a small piece of calcium to the water. His teacher tells him that an exothermic reaction will take place.

a Explain what he should expect to happen to the thermometer.

b Write a word equation for the reaction between calcium and water.

4 Why is it dangerous to add large pieces of sodium to water?

5 White sugar is a carbohydrate, containing carbon together with hydrogen and oxygen in the same proportions as in water. Concentrated sulphuric acid is a powerful dehydrating agent. When a little of this acid is added to sugar in a test-tube, the mixture turns into a black solid and steam is given out, pushing the black solid up the test-tube.

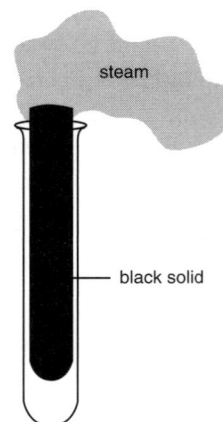

a What do you think the black solid is?

b What type of chemical reaction has taken place? What is the evidence for your answer?

Continued ▶

1.7 Energy transfer (2)

6 The reaction between an acid and an alkali is exothermic. In some acid-alkali titrations, a sensitive thermometer can be used instead of an indicator.

$10 \, cm^3$ of an alkali are measured into a conical flask and its temperature is measured.

An acid (at the same initial temperature as the alkali) is added a little at a time and thermometer readings are taken for each addition. They are shown in the table.

total volume of acid added in cm^3	temperature in °C
0.0	18.30
3.0	18.55
5.0	19.00
7.0	19.60
9.0	20.15
11.0	20.65
13.0	21.50
15.0	20.70
17.0	20.20
19.0	19.70

a Plot these results on a graph, with the volume on the y-axis.

b Draw two 'best fit' lines and find where they intersect. This is where the end-point is.

c The ionic equation for this reaction is:

$$H^+(aq) + OH^-(aq) \rightarrow H_2O(l)$$

When bonds are formed, energy is released.

From this information, suggest why the graph has the shape you have plotted.

7 In a chemical reaction, energy is needed to break the existing bonds in the reactants. Energy is given out as new bonds are formed in making the products. If the energy given out is greater than that taken in, the reaction is exothermic.

a Here is some data about bond energies in methane and oxygen gas.

bond	kJ
C-H	435
O=O	498

When a mole of methane burns, it needs two moles of oxygen.

$$CH_4 + 2O_2 \rightarrow CO_2 + 2H_2O$$

This can be written as

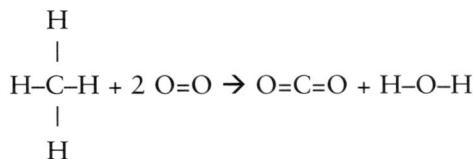

$$H-\underset{\underset{H}{|}}{\overset{\overset{H}{|}}{C}}-H + 2\, O=O \rightarrow O=C=O + H-O-H$$

   i How many C–H bonds are in CH_4?
   ii How much energy is needed to break them?
   iii How many O=O bonds are in $2O_2$?
   iv How much energy is needed to break them?
   v What is the total amount of energy needed to break the bonds in CH_4 and $2O_2$?

b Here is some data about bond energies in carbon dioxide and water.

bond	kJ
C=O	805
H–O	464

   i How many C=O bonds are there in CO_2?
   ii How much energy is released in making CO_2?
   iii How many H–O bonds are there in $2H_2O$?
   iv How much energy is released in making $2H_2O$?
   v What is the total amount of energy needed to make the bonds in CO_2 and H_2O?

c Compare your answers in **a** and **b** and decide whether the data agrees with the reaction being exothermic.

8 The energy changes in a reaction can be shown by an energy level diagram. Copy and complete the two diagrams below to show

a an exothermic reaction

b an endothermic reaction.

On each, write down the label 'products' and show where you measure the exothermic or endothermic change.

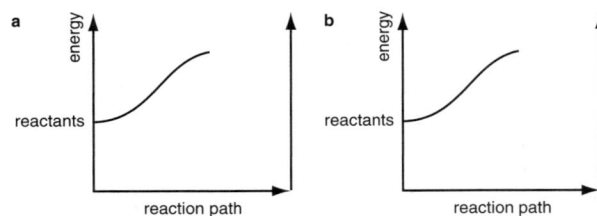

1.8 Extracting minerals

Key points

- Extracting minerals from the Earth's crust is vital if we are to provide raw materials for the construction, road and metal extraction industries.

- Care must be taken, however, to minimise the impact that this extraction has on the environment.
- This section considers the extraction of limestone.

1 Here are some statements to do with extraction, processing and uses of calcium carbonate. Some of the keywords (printed in **bold**) have been jumbled up. Sort out the correct spelling of these words. (The number 2 shows that the letters make two words.)

Calcium carbonate is found in the rock known as **eeilmnost**. Calcium carbonate is also found naturally in **achkl** and **abelmr**.

This is extracted from its deposits in **aeiqrrsu**.

The process can cause **dstu** to be made.

People living close to the process can also experience **eiillnnooopstu (2)** from the **acehimnry** and **eiloonpssx**.

It is transported in **aeehilorrsvy (2)** for further processing.

This means that a good **adeknoorrtw (2)** is needed, not narrow country **aelns**.

Much of it can be taken to a **eiikllmn** where it is heated in air and **aefglsu (2)** to produce calcium oxide known as **ceiiklmqu (2)**.

This can be used by **aefmrrs** to spread on **defils** which are too **accdii**.

When calcium oxide reacts with water there is a highly **ceehimortx** reaction which can even turn some of the water into **aemst**.

The water converts the calcium oxide into **accdehiilmoruxy (2)** known as slaked lime.

Some of this type of calcium carbonate is used to build **adors** and to make **cement**, used in **amorrt**.

a A road-maker needs to use pieces of rocks which, when mixed with tar, produce a firm surface which does not wear out tyres but gives good grip.

Which of the six types of rock shown in the table below:

i would be the easiest to crush to make a smooth surface?

ii would be the most difficult to make into small pieces?

iii would cause the most tyre wear in dry conditions?

iv gives least grip to tyres in wet weather?

b In making a motorway, the foundations have to be strong to resist the pounding from continuous heavy traffic, yet smooth enough to be able to have a level tar and stone top surface.

In a predominantly dry climate, a road-maker decides to use a mixture of gabbro, flint, quartzite and limestone for the foundations and a quartzite with limestone mixture in the tarred surface.

Explain why these rocks were chosen.

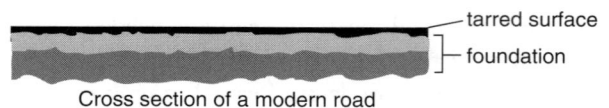

Cross section of a modern road

2

rock type	strength against crushing	strength against impact	tyre wear	
			when dry	when wet
flint	9	24	24	26
gabbro	7	31	26	22
schist	14	15	20	16
quartzite	28	20	26	24
sandstone	9	16	24	12
limestone	2	0.5	18	1

2.1 Extraction of metals

Key points

- Metals are extracted from ores.
- Less reactive metals are extracted by reduction using carbon or carbon monoxide.
- More reactive metals are extracted by electrolysis.
- Some metals are recycled.

1 Here is a table showing some metals with their approximate relative prices per kilogram and an estimate of the number of years that known reserves of their ores will last.

metal	price	years
aluminium	£3	60
chromium	£5	350
copper	£4	70
gold	£9000	27
iron	£1	302
silver	£150	30
tin	£10	40
zinc	£2	36

a Starting with the cheapest metal, iron, draw a bar chart to show this information. Use two bars per metal, one for price and one for years. Is there any trend visible? Can you draw any general conclusions about the prices and the number of years that known reserves will last?

b Here are three main factors which affect the price of a metal:

i its abundance in the Earth's crust

ii the quality of the ore

iii the cost of reduction.

Explain why these are so important.

c State three other factors which affect the cost of a metal.

d Iron makes up about 5% of the Earth's crust. Aluminium is even more abundant. But aluminium is more expensive than iron. Why do you think this is so?

IDEAS AND EVIDENCE

2 The information in question 1 shows that the known reserves of some metals will run out in a few years' time. The phrase 'known reserves' means the amounts of ore which are known to be worth mining at present production costs. What should be done as these reserves are used up?

3 Explain the meaning of words printed in **bold** in the passage which follows.

Many metals are **combined** with oxygen or sulphur in the Earth's surface. These are ores which have to be mined or quarried. The ore often has to be **concentrated** before the metal can be **extracted** from it by **reduction**.

4 This table shows where some metals are found in the reactivity series, and the method used to extract them from their ores. The most reactive metals are at the top.

metal	method of extraction
potassium	
sodium	electrolysis
calcium	
aluminium	
zinc	reduction using carbon
iron	or carbon monoxide
lead	
silver	found uncombined,
gold	then purified

What method would you expect to be used to extract the following metals from their ores:

a magnesium (between calcium and aluminium in the reactivity series)

b nickel (between iron and lead in the reactivity series)

c platinum (between silver and gold in the reactivity series)?

5 Chromium is extracted from chromium(III) oxide, Cr_2O_3, by heating it with aluminium. Chromium and aluminium oxide are produced.

a Write a balanced equation for this reaction.

b Which substance is being reduced?

c Which substance is being oxidised?

d What can you conclude about the position of aluminium compared with chromium in the reactivity series?

2.2 Extraction of iron

Key points

- Iron is extracted from its ores using the blast furnace.

- The raw materials for this process are iron ore, coke, limestone and air.
- Slag is produced as a by-product.

---

1 Here is a diagram of a blast furnace used to extract iron from its main ore, haematite.

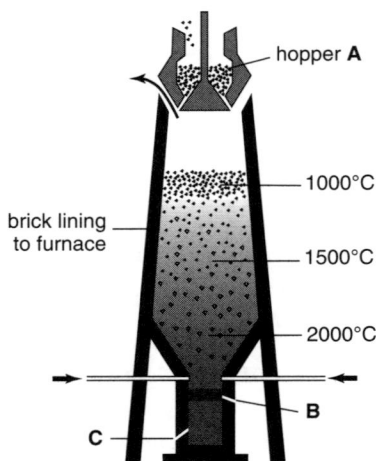

hopper **A**

1000°C

brick lining to furnace

1500°C

2000°C

B

C

a Copy the diagram and label it to show:
  i what is loaded through the hopper at A
  ii what is tapped off at the base at B and C
  iii where the hot air enters
  iv where the waste gases come out.

b What is the name of the main compound in:
  i haematite
  ii limestone?

c i What is coke made from?
  ii What is the coke used for in this process?

d The hopper has to be 'gas-tight' so that nothing escapes through it. Why is this so important?

e How does a blast furnace get its name?

f Why is **hot** air used?

g i What is the main impurity in **iron ore**?
  ii How is it removed?

h i What is the name given to iron from a blast furnace?
  ii What is the main impurity in this sort of iron?
  iii What effect does it have on this iron?

i Years ago, there were huge slag heaps near iron works. What is 'slag' and what have the slag heaps been used for?

---

2 Write equations for the following reactions which occur in a blast furnace.

a formation of carbon dioxide

b formation of carbon monoxide

c reaction of iron(III) oxide with carbon monoxide

d reaction of calcium carbonate with silicon(IV) oxide

---

3 The iron from a blast furnace is heated in a furnace with more oxygen. A carefully controlled amount of carbon is then added, together with traces of other metals such as chromium. The result is a steel.

a Explain why these elements are added.

b What is the general name given to this type of mixture?

c Why are steels much less brittle than 'pig iron'?

IDEAS AND EVIDENCE

4 Here is a map of England and Wales showing where some of the major coalfields and ironworks used to be sited.

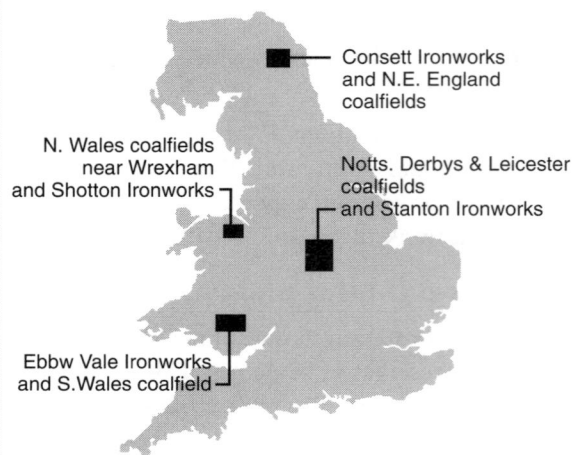

Consett Ironworks and N.E. England coalfields

N. Wales coalfields near Wrexham and Shotton Ironworks

Notts. Derbys & Leicester coalfields and Stanton Ironworks

Ebbw Vale Ironworks and S.Wales coalfield

Suggest why the ironworks were sited near the coalfields.

2.3 **Extraction of aluminium**

> ### Key points
>
> - Bauxite, the main ore of aluminium, contains aluminium oxide.
> - Aluminium is made by electrolysis of aluminium oxide.

1 Aluminium is the most abundant metal found in the Earth's crust. Explain why, in the 19th century, it was even more expensive than gold or silver.

2 Here is a diagram of an electrolysis cell in which aluminium is extracted.

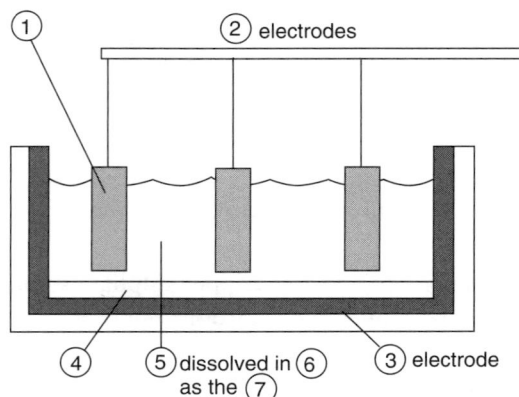

The letters in the labels below have been mixed up. Unravel them to give the correct labels.

1 abcnor bcklos
2 eiiopstv
3 aeeigntv
4 aiilmmnuu
5 aiilmmnuu ediox
6 ceilorty
7 elmnot ceeellortty

3 Aluminium is extracted from the ore called bauxite, though aluminium is most commonly found in clay.

a What does the word **ore** mean?

b Why is aluminium extracted from bauxite instead of clay?

4 The process uses a series of cells with a 5 volts d.c.(direct current) supply of electricity. Explain why an a.c. (alternating current) supply would be useless in this electrolysis.

5 Explain why the purified aluminium oxide has to be dissolved in cryolite before being electrolysed.

6 The molten aluminium is extracted from the cell by syphoning it into an evacuated container, then letting it cool before it is cast into ingots. Aluminium is very high in the reactivity series.

Suggest why it is not just run out from the base of the cell.

7 The positive carbon electrodes burn away during the electrolysis process. The gas formed is dangerous and is piped away to be burnt and used as a fuel in the extraction plant.

a What is the name of the gas produced?

b Write an equation for the reaction between this gas and oxygen.

c Suggest where the heat produced in **b** could be used in the electrolysis process.

8 In the electrolysis cell, the electrolyte contains Al^{3+} and O^{2-} ions. Write half equations (ion/electrons) to show what happens:

a at the positive electrode

b at the negative electrode.

IDEAS AND EVIDENCE

9 There are no bauxite or cryolite deposits in this country. Our supplies come from as far away as Australia. The main extraction plant for our aluminium used to be on the slopes of Ben Nevis (Scotland) where there was a hydro-electricity scheme. These days aluminium is extracted near Holyhead (Angelsey, Wales) near a nuclear power station. Both sites are near deep-water harbours.

Suggest why:

a these sites were chosen,

b the bauxite is purified before the ore is imported into this country.

2.4 **Purification of copper**

- Electrical wiring requires copper of high purity.

- Copper is purified by electrolysis.

1 This word search is about the purification of copper. Answers may be horizontal or vertical, forwards or backwards, but not diagonal.

W	A	T	E	A	N	I	O	N	Q	U	E
P	E	S	C	B	A	C	D	P	N	C	L
O	P	A	O	J	G	A	N	I	O	R	E
S	U	L	P	H	A	T	E	P	I	E	C
I	R	T	P	K	T	I	L	E	T	T	T
T	E	G	E	T	I	O	N	S	U	A	R
I	T	H	R	U	V	N	K	W	L	W	O
V	A	D	I	R	E	C	T	I	O	V	N
E	L	E	C	T	R	O	L	Y	S	I	S

Clues

a Substance put into the cell (6,8,8)
b Principle of method (12)
c These conduct electricity in liquids (4)
d Cu^{2+} is an example (6)
e Attracted to positive electrode (5)
f Cu^{2+} travels to this electrode (8)
g Electrode made of crude copper (8)
h The type of current used (6)
i This copper is used for the negative electrode (4)
j Copper sulphate is an example (4)
k Type of liquid in the cell (8)
l Copper carries water in them (5)
m Conducts current in copper wire (9)

2 Try to think of four reasons why copper is a good material from which to make water pipes. What are the advantages of making water pipes from copper instead of iron?

3

a Copper is an excellent material from which to make electrical wiring. Apart from its ability to conduct electricity well, what properties make it a good choice of metal to use?

b Overhead 'high tension' electrical cables use a central core of steel with an outer sheath of aluminium. If copper is such a good conductor, suggest why copper is not used for these outdoor cables.

c Suggest why the copper used for electrical conduction has to be very pure (99.99%).

4 In Canada, copper occurs in huge boulders on the shores of the Great Lakes. It is possible to build an electrolysis cell round it and extract it 'on site'.

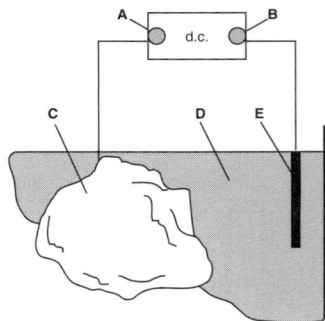

Copy the diagram and label **A** to **E** using terms from this list.

water	copper sulphate solution
impure copper	carbon
pure copper	positive
negative	

5

a In the electrolysis of copper sulphate solution to produce pure copper, write an ionic equation to show what happens:

  i at the negative electrode
  ii at the positive electrode.

b Explain why the electrolysis of copper sulphate solution involves reduction and oxidation. Show where these reactions occur, illustrating your answer with ionic equations.

6 The main ore of copper is converted into a 'matte' which contains Cu_2S and the impurity FeS. This is removed by heating with oxygen and silicon dioxide. Once the iron is removed, the copper(I) sulphide is oxidised to 'blister' copper, from which the pure copper is extracted.

a Balance the equations for these reactions.

  i $FeS + O_2 + SiO_2 \rightarrow FeSiO_3 + SO_2$
  ii $Cu_2S + O_2 \rightarrow Cu + SO_2$

b Suggest how the sulphur dioxide released could then usefully be used.

2.5 The transition metals

Key points

- Transition metals have low reactivities.
- They have high melting points and high densities.
- Most compounds of transition metals are coloured.

1 Silver and gold are called 'precious metals'. They are quite scarce in the Earth's crust. They can be polished and do not corrode like iron.

Draw a poster about the uses of **either** silver **or** gold, to include reasons for the uses.

2 Use the Periodic Table on page 81 to find out where the transition metals are.

Copy the table below and fill in the symbols and atomic numbers of the transition metals listed.

name	symbol	at. no.	name	symbol	at. no.
chromium			zinc		
manganese			silver		
iron			tungsten		
nickel			gold		
copper			vanadium		

3 Here are some properties of a selection of metals and their compounds.

Metal A – has no reaction with dilute hydrochloric acid or water; produces blue/green salts; forms two oxides, one black and the other pinky red.

Metal B – reacts with dilute acids; has no reaction with cold water; forms two hydroxides, one green and the other brown; forms two different chlorides, BCl_2 and BCl_3.

Metal C – acts as a catalyst in making margarine from hydrocarbons; is used in making coins; has no reaction with water; forms a green carbonate.

Metal D – reacts readily with water; can be chopped up with a knife; its simple compounds are white.

From this information suggest which three of the metals **A, B ,C** and **D** are likely to be transition metals. Suggest what type of metal the non-transition metal is. (You are not expected to identify any of the metals.)

4 Choose names from the table of transition metals in question 2 to fit the following statements.

The names can be used once, more than once or not at all.

a Catalyst in the Haber process for making ammonia.
b Extracted from a blue salt in solution by electrolysis.
c Used with iron and nickel to make stainless steel.
d Used to make water pipes.
e Used with copper to make brass.
f Used as the filament in electric light bulbs.
g The most commonly used metal.
h These **two** metals are used together to make our 'silver' coins.
i Corrodes badly in water containing dissolved oxygen.

5 Chromium is an important metal in widely different ways. It is used in alloys and is an essential element in the human diet where it assists sugar metabolism. It can be extracted by displacing chromium from chromium(III) oxide by heating it with aluminium, or by electrolysis of a solution of an alum containing chromium(III) sulphate.

a i What does this suggest about the relative positions of aluminium and chromium in the reactivity series?

  ii Complete and balance the equation for the reaction.

$$Cr_2O_3 \quad + \quad Al \rightarrow \underline{\hspace{2cm}} + \underline{\hspace{2cm}}$$

b i During electrolysis of chromium(III) sulphate solution, chromium is deposited on the cathode.

Copy and complete this ionic equation for the reaction at the negative electrode.

$$Cr^{3+} \quad \rightarrow \quad Cr$$

  ii Oxygen is discharged at the positive electrode. Copy and complete this ionic equation for the reaction at the positive electrode.

$$2O^{2-} \quad \rightarrow \quad O_2$$

  iii When magnesium sulphate solution is electrolysed, hydrogen is given off at the negative electrode.

Put the three elements chromium, magnesium and hydrogen in order of reactivity, with the most reactive first.

3.1 Atomic structure

Key points

- Atoms are made of protons, neutrons and electrons.
- Atoms of one element all have the same number of protons.
- Nearly all the mass of an atom is from protons and neutrons.

---

1 Copy and complete the following sentences, using words from the list to fill in the spaces. Words may be used more than once.

atomic	charge	electrons
mass	negative	neutrons
nucleus	positive	protons

The number of protons in an atom of an element is known as the _____ number of that element.

A neutral atom contains equal numbers of _____ and _____ . The mass number of an atom is found by adding together the number of protons and _____ . The number of neutrons in an atom is found by taking away the _____ number from the _____ number. The _____ and neutrons are found in the central part of an atom, called the nucleus. Electrons are found spinning in space outside the _____ . The masses of individual _____ and _____ are the same. It takes about 2000 _____ to equal the mass of a single proton. That is why nearly all the mass of an atom is found in the _____ . Protons and _____ have opposite charge. Each of the _____ carries one positive charge and each of the _____ carries one _____ charge. There is no _____ on a neutron. Some atoms have isotopes because they have a different number of _____ in the _____ . This means that the _____ number is still the same but the different isotopes will have different _____ numbers.

---

2 The atomic number, Z, and mass number, A, of an atom of an element **M** can be shown as:

$$_Z^A M$$

Work out the number of protons, neutrons and electrons in the atoms shown in the table below.

atom	protons	neutrons	electrons
$_2^4$He			
$_4^9$Be			
$_5^{11}$B			
$_6^{12}$C			
$_6^{14}$C			

---

3 The atomic number, Z, mass number, A, and change of a particle of an element **M** are shown as:

$$_Z^A M^{2+}$$

Work out the number of protons, neutrons and electrons in the particles shown in the table below.

particle	protons	neutrons	electrons
$_3^7$Li$^+$			
$_8^{16}$O^{2-}			
$_{13}^{27}$Al^{3+}			
$_{15}^{31}$P^{3-}			
$_{17}^{37}$Cl			

---

4 In every four chlorine atoms, three have a mass number of 35 and one has a mass number of 37.

So, the relative atomic mass of chlorine is

$$\frac{3 \times 35}{4} + \frac{1 \times 37}{4} = 35.5$$

Work out the relative atomic masses of:

a copper, if seven atoms in every ten have a mass number of 63 and three atoms in every ten have a mass number of 65,

b gallium, if six atoms in every ten have a mass number of 69 and four atoms in every ten have a mass number of 71.

3.2 Finding a pattern

Key points

- Groups of elements have similar properties.
- Elements can be listed in order of increasing atomic number.

- Elements with similar properties occur at regular intervals.
- In the Periodic Table similar elements are in Groups.

IDEAS AND EVIDENCE

1 The table shows some data about the elements found in the second period of the modern Periodic Table.

element	group number	boiling point in °C	density in g/cm³	atomic number	relative atomic mass
lithium	1		0.53	3	7
beryllium	2		1.85	4	9
boron	3		2.34	5	11
carbon	4		3.51	6	12
nitrogen	5			7	14
oxygen	6			8	16
fluorine	7			9	19
neon	8			10	20

a   Copy the table, and write in the boiling points of the elements using the data on page 83.

Draw a bar graph with the elements in the order lithium to neon across the base line, to show the atomic number and the relative atomic mass of each element. Write the Group number under each element name.

b   Draw bar graphs with the elements lithium to carbon across the base line, to show the boiling point and the density. Write the atomic number under the name of each element. What trend can you see in these bar graphs?

c   Draw the same type of bar graph for the elements nitrogen to neon. What trend can you see in these bar graphs?

d   Can you suggest what is the important difference in structure between the elements lithium to carbon compared with nitrogen to neon?

2 In 1798, Lavoisier produced a list of substances which he thought were elements. They included light, heat, oxygen, nitrogen, phosphorus, cobalt, platinum, alumina (aluminium oxide) and silica (silicon oxide).

a   Which of the above list are now known to be single elements?

b   Why did the discovery of electrolysis around 1800 make a classification of elements a little easier?

c   In 1869, Mendeléev produced a Periodic Table on which the modern one is based. What was the basis on which he put the elements into an order? Suggest what assumptions he had to make.

d   Using a modern Periodic Table, look up the elements potassium and argon. What do you notice about the sequence of their relative atomic masses compared with other elements? What is the principle by which elements are put into sequence in a modern Periodic Table? Why did Mendeléev not use this principle?

3 From your knowledge of the trends in the groups of the Periodic Table, suggest in which group each of these elements will be found.

a   **X** is a solid. Its relative atomic mass is just below 140. It reacts very readily with water and forms an ionic chloride of formula XCl_2.

b   **Y** is a solid. It is stored under oil. When put onto water it reacts very violently and explodes. Its sulphate is ionic and has the formula Y_2SO_4.

c   **Z** is a silvery-black solid. It is not very soluble in water but dissolves easily in covalent solvents. On warming solid **Z** turns to a purple vapour. It forms a compound of formula KZ.

3.3 Elements in the Periodic Table

1 Use the Periodic Table on page 81. On a sheet of A4 paper make a copy of its outline shape and use different colours to show the important areas as follows.

a Draw a line down on the left of, and underneath, each of these elements so that it looks like a 'stair-case': B(5), Si(14) As(33), Te(52) At(85). Label all the elements to the **left** of this line as **metals** [to include the lanthanides Ce(58) to Lu(71)and actinides (99) to (112)].

b Draw a line across the top of B(3) to Ne(10), then down to Rn(86) and back under At(85). Label all these elements to the right of the 'stair-case' as **non-metals** (to include H and He).

c Colour in the vertical Groups to show:

  i Group 1 – alkali metals
  ii Group 2 – alkali earths
  iii Group 7 – halogens
  iv Group 0 – noble gases
  v elements Sc(21) to Zn(30) and those underneath – transition metals.

2 Here is another form of the Periodic Table, designed by Zmaczynski.

Find and label the same Groups as in question **1c**.

```
                    H He
              Li Be B C N O F Ne
              Na Mg  Al Si P S Cl Ar

      K  Ca Sc  Ti  V Cr Mn Fe Co Ni Cu Zn Ga Ge As Se Br Kr
      Rb Sr  Y     Zr Nb Mo Te Ru Rh Pd Ag Cd In Sn Sb Te  I Xe

Cs Ba La  Ce Pr Nd PmSmEuGdTbDy Ho Er Tm Yb Lu Hf Ta  W  Re Os  Ir  Pt  Au Hg Tl Pb Bi Po At Rn
Fr Ra Ac     Th Pa U Np Pu Am Cm Bk Cf Es Fm Md No Lr Rf Ha Sg Ns Hs Mt 110 111 112
```

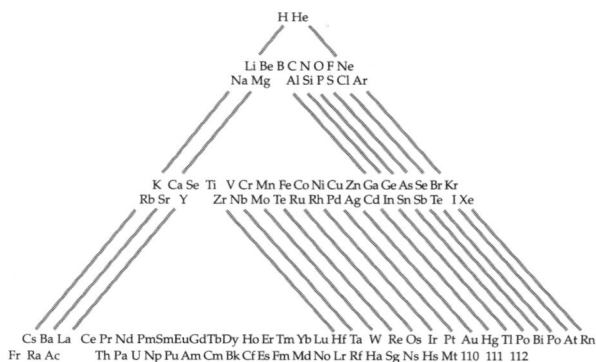

3 Rubidium (Rb) is in the same Group as sodium and potassium. How will it react with:

a water

b air (oxygen)?

c Explain how rubidium should be stored.

d Write equations for the reactions in **a** and **b**.

e Write down the molecular formula for:

  i rubidium chloride
  ii rubidium carbonate
  iii rubidium sulphate.

4 Astatine is below iodine in Group 7. From your knowledge of the other halogens, suggest what would happen if:

a chlorine gas were bubbled through sodium astatide solution

b astatine were shaken with sodium bromide solution.

5 Hydrogen is a non-metal but often acts like a metal in chemical reactions. For example, it can be displaced from an acid by a reactive metal and its ions are discharged at the negative electrode during electrolysis. Both of these are examples of oxidation and reduction.

a Write an ionic equation for the reaction between zinc and hydrochloric acid. Explain what is being oxidised and what is being reduced in this reaction.

b Write an ionic equation for the discharge of hydrogen ions at the negative electrode during electrolysis. Explain why this is an example of reduction.

IDEAS AND EVIDENCE

6 Iron is a transition metal. Transition metals usually have the following properties.

1. They form coloured compounds.

2. They can have variable combining powers.

3. They can act as catalysts.

What evidence is there that iron is a transition metal?

3.4 Electron arrangement (1)

Key points

- Electrons are arranged in shells.
- Each shell holds a maximum number of electrons.
- The number of electrons in the outer shell is the same as the Group number of the element in the Periodic Table.

1 In an atom, the number of protons in the nucleus is balanced by the number of electrons in the shells around the nucleus. For the first 20 elements, the first shell can contain two electrons, the second eight electrons, the third eight electrons and the next two electrons are found in the fourth shell. The electron arrangement can be found from the atomic number, e.g. potassium (19) has the electron arrangement (2,8,8,1).

Copy and complete the table for the named elements.

element	atomic number	electron arrangement
helium	2	
beryllium	4	
carbon	6	
nitrogen	7	
aluminium	13	
argon	18	
calcium	20	

2 Choose **one** of the following elements and produce a poster which shows the protons and neutrons in the nucleus and the electrons in the shells for one atom of that element.

7	19	39
Li	F	K
3	9	19

3 Find the elements lithium, sodium and potassium in the Periodic Table.

a Write down the electronic arrangement for each element.

b In which Group of the Periodic Table are they found?

c What do their electron arrangements have in common?

d What kind of ion do they all produce in a chemical reaction?

4 The alkali earths in Group 2 all react with water.

a What are the products of the reaction?

b By reference to the electrons present, suggest why the vigour of the reaction increases moving down the Group.

5 In some of their compounds, nitrogen, oxygen and fluorine can form ions.

a Work out the electronic arrangements for N^{3-}, O^{2-} and F^- ions.

b What do they have in common?

c Suggest what the rule is about gain or loss of electrons for many elements when they form ions.

6

a Write down the electronic arrangement for chlorine.

b Explain why chlorine forms ions with the formula Cl^- and not Cl^+ or Cl^{2-}.

Continued ▶

3.4 Electron arrangement (2)

⟨7⟩ Copy and complete the table below which shows atoms and ions of some elements.

symbol	name of element	species	number of: protons	neutrons	electrons	electronic arrangement
$^{7}_{3}\text{Li}$		atom				
$^{16}_{8}\text{O}^{2-}$		ion				
^{14}N		atom	7			
F^{-}			9	10		
^{28}Si		atom			14	
S^{2-}		ion	16	16		
^{80}Br		atom				(2,8,18,7)
Cl^{-}				20		(2,8,8)

3.5 Elements in the Periodic Table

Key points

- Group 1 contains the most reactive metal elements.

- There is a trend in physical properties in this Group.
- Reactivity increases down the Group.

---

1 This table shows some of the physical properties of the alkali metals in Group 1.

period	alkali metal	density in g/cm³	melting point in °C
2	lithium	0.53	181
3	sodium	0.57	98
4	potassium	0.86	63
5	rubidium	1.53	39
6	caesium	1.88	29

a Draw a bar graph with the elements on the horizontal axis to show the densities of these metals. Under each element, write down the period in which it is found. What trend does the bar graph show?

b Draw a second bar graph to show the melting points. What trend does this bar graph show?

c The density of water is $1\,g/cm^3$.

What physical difference would you expect to see when comparing the reaction of potassium and rubidium with water?

2 State whether each of the following statements is true or false.

a Potassium hydroxide has a pH value of about 3.

b Group 1 metals combine with chlorine using ionic bonds.

c Group 1 metals are extracted by methods using electrolysis.

d All alkali metals float on water.

e The reaction between alkali metals and water is exothermic.

3 Suggest why sodium is not used in making coins.

4 When lithium reacts with water it bubbles gently on the surface of the water. The products are lithium hydroxide and hydrogen. Rubidium reacts explosively with water to produce rubidium hydroxide and hydrogen.

a How many electrons are in the outer shell of each of these elements?

b Which shells are these electrons in?

c What charge will be on each of their ions?

d Suggest why there is a difference in the vigour of the reactions of lithium and rubidium with water.

e Write a word equation for the reaction of lithium with water.

f Write a balanced equation for the reaction of lithium with water.

g Write an ionic equation for the reaction of lithium with water.

h Why does lithium not normally produce a Li^- ion?

i Write the formulae for the following compounds.

  i lithium bromide
  ii lithium sulphate
  iii lithium nitrate
  iv lithium carbonate
  v lithium oxide
  vi lithium sulphide

5 Ben knows that:

- sodium is very high in the reactivity series
- a metal high in the series will displace a metal lower in the series from a solution of a salt.

Ben drops a small piece of sodium into a solution of copper(II) sulphate. He expects to see a deposit of red–orange copper appear, but instead he sees many bubbles of gas. The solution gets warmer and has a pH value of about 11. Explain what has happened.

6 Explain why would it be very dangerous to drop a piece of potassium into hydrochloric acid.

7 When a Group 1 alkali solution is added to a solution of a transition metal salt, a coloured precipitate of the metal hydroxide is formed.

a Write balanced equations for these reactions.

  i copper(II) sulphate + sodium hydroxide
  ii iron(II) chloride + potassium hydroxide
  iii zinc nitrate + lithium hydroxide

b Write ionic equations for these reactions.

3.6 **The halogens**

Key points

- The halogens (Group 7) are very reactive non-metals.

- There are patterns in their properties down the Group.

halogen	relative atomic mass	colour	melting point in °C	boiling point in °C
fluorine	19	yellow		
chlorine	35.5	green		
bromine	80	red-brown		
iodine	127	silvery-grey		

1 Use the information on page 83 to copy and complete the table above. Putting the halogens along the horizontal axis, draw a bar graph to show:

a their melting points

b their boiling points.

c What trends do the bar graphs show?

2 Astatine was first made in 1940. It is an unstable radioactive element in Group 7, immediately below iodine. It's atom has 32 more protons and 51 more neutrons than an atom of iodine.

a Work out the relative atomic mass of astatine.

b Suggest what it looks like at room temperature.

c Estimate its melting point.

3 Produce a pie-chart to show the uses of chlorine from the following information.

   Making plastics e.g. polyvinylchloride: 27%

   Making hydrochloric acid and bleaches: 13%

   Making organic solvents and other organic compounds: 33%

   Making drugs and water purification chemicals: 21%

   Other uses: 6%

4 Fluorine, chlorine and bromine exist as small molecules each containing two atoms covalently linked together in the molecule. This covalent bond is a strong bond. How can you explain that fluorine and chlorine are gases and that bromine easily turns into a gas?

5 Some iron wool is heated in a test-tube in the presence of chlorine as shown in the diagram. As soon as a reaction starts, the heat source is

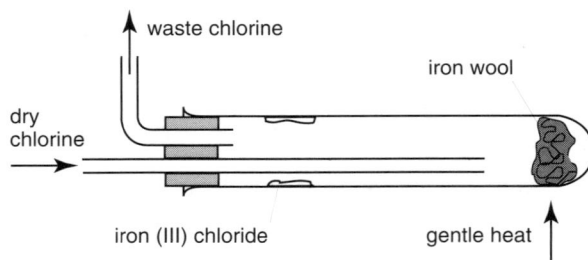

waste chlorine

iron wool

dry chlorine

iron (III) chloride

gentle heat

removed. A brown gas is formed which solidifies in the cooler part of the test-tube. The iron continues to glow whilst the reaction goes on.

a What is the name given to the change from gas directly to a solid?

b The reaction produces iron(III) chloride as the only product. Write a word equation and a balanced symbol equation for this reaction.

c The iron continues to glow after the heat source has been removed. What does this indicate about the reaction?

d What precaution is essential if this experiment is to be carried out in a chemistry lesson?

e The reaction using fluorine and iron is much more vigorous. What would you expect if bromine was used instead of chlorine?

6 Decide whether reactions occur between the following substances. If there is a reaction, write a word equation (■), a balanced equation (◆) and an ionic equation (◇) for each reaction.

a bromine with potassium iodide solution

b chlorine with sodium bromide solution

c iodine with potassium chloride

d explain why these reactions are 'redox' reactions.

3.7 Uses of chlorine

Key points

- Chlorine is used to sterilise water.
- Bleach is made using chlorine.
- Chlorine is used to make chlorofluorocarbons.

- There are hazards involved when using chlorine and other halogens.

1 Decide whether these each of these statements about chlorine is true or false.

a It is used as a fuel.

b It is found in salt.

c It removes sand from water.

d It kills bacteria in water.

e It is used to make some plastics.

2 In this word search the answers may be horizontal or vertical, forwards or backwards, but not diagonal. Clues are given below.

C	F	U	M	E	N	R	L	A
H	A	L	O	G	E	N	B	S
L	B	I	U	S	A	K	R	O
O	L	G	C	O	M	S	O	D
R	E	H	F	B	R	O	M	I
I	A	T	C	P	F	I	I	U
N	C	G	S	E	V	E	N	M
E	H	I	O	D	I	N	E	E

Clues

a Short for chlorofluorocarbons (4)

b Astatine is the radioactive one (7)

c Used in swimming baths (8)

d Has an atomic number of 35 (7)

e Astatine is at the bottom of this Group (5)

f Extracted from sea-weed (6)

g Stain-remover (6)

h Physical state of chlorine (3)

i An angry gas in a ..... cupboard? (4)

j Short for trichlorophenol (3)

k Reacts with silver bromide (5)

l Found with chlorine in salt (6)

3 Unravel the words in bold type and copy out this paragraph with the correct words in place.

Chlorine is a very **inooopssu** element. It kills **aabceirt** in water, which might cause diseases like **acehlor** and **dhiopty**. So it is used to **eeiilrsst** water in **giimmnsw** pools and **dgiiknnr** water supplies.

4 When chlorine is added to sodium hydroxide solution a bleach is produced.

chlorine + sodium hydroxide →
 sodium chloride + sodium chlorate (I) + water

a Which of the products acts as a bleach?

b Which of the following is this bleach used for?
- To kill bacteria in toilets
- To remove colour from dyed materials
- To sterilise drinking water

c Balance this equation for the reaction:

$Cl_2 + NaOH \rightarrow NaCl + NaClO + H_2O$

5 If bleach is mixed with an acid, chlorine gas is set free. Limescale remover contains an acid. When limescale is treated with the acid, carbon dioxide gas is set free.

a Explain why it is dangerous to put bleach and limescale remover into a toilet at the same time.

b Suppose the acid in a limescale remover is HX. Copy and complete this equation for the reaction with the limescale (calcium carbonate).

$HX + CaCO_3 \rightarrow CaX_2 + CO_2 + H_2O$

c Copy and complete this equation for the reaction of limescale remover HX and bleach.

$HX + NaClO \rightarrow NaX + Cl_2 + H_2O$

IDEAS AND EVIDENCE

6 Chlorofluorocarbons (CFCs) are unreactive compounds which were used in aerosol sprays and refrigerators. Their use is now banned by law because they damage an important protective layer in our atmosphere.

a What is the name of this layer?

b From what does this layer protect us?

c Over which parts of the Earth's surface is this layer thought to be the most damaged?

d If this layer becomes too damaged, how can we protect ourselves?

e If we do not protect ourselves sufficiently what could the result be?

3.8 Sodium chloride

Key points

- Sodium and chlorine react together to make sodium chloride.
- Sodium chloride is used to make sodium hydroxide.
- Rock salt is used to de-ice winter roads.

1 Most of our salt comes from deposits found underground in Cheshire. It can be extracted by one of two methods.

- By driving lorries underground and carrying it out as 'rock salt'.
- By pumping water down pipes to dissolve the salt and pumping the solution back to the surface as 'brine' from which salt crystals can form.

a Why do you think that large scale deposits of salt are not found on the surface?

b Where do you think these underground salt deposits came from?

c The 'rock salt' can be brownish in colour instead of the expected white colour. What could cause this?

d Which of the two methods of extraction is likely to give the purest form of salt? Give your reason.

2 Sodium chloride is a white salt which melts at $801\,^{\circ}C$. It is soluble in water but its solubility does not increase much even at high temperature. It can be made by passing chlorine over hot sodium, but it is easier to extract it from sea-water or underground deposits.

a Copy and complete the balanced equation for the reaction between sodium and chlorine.

$$Na + Cl_2 \rightarrow NaCl$$

b The atomic number for sodium is 11 and the atomic number for chlorine is 17. Write down the electron arrangements for these two elements.

c Explain what sort of bond is made when sodium combines with chlorine.

d Why does this reaction have to be carried out in a fume cupboard?

e In hot climates, salt can be obtained by leaving sea-water in large pans in the sunshine. Explain what the sunshine does. Why would this method not be very successful in a cold climate such as Iceland or Norway?

3 When salt solution is electrolysed, it produces chlorine, hydrogen and sodium hydroxide. The process is called the **chlor-alkali** process.

a Why is the term 'alkali' included in the name?

b The process is carried out in a membrane cell. Here is a diagram of it.

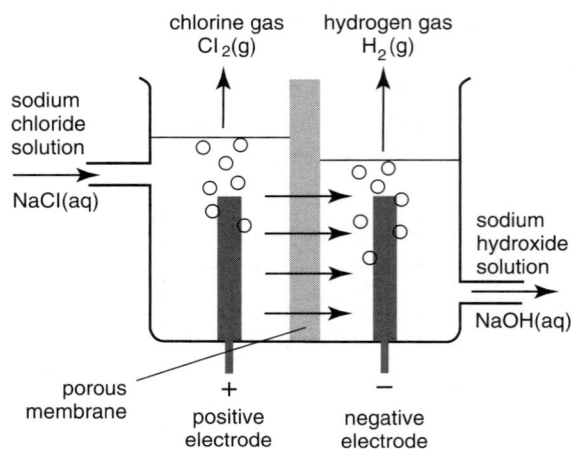

The membrane is 'ion-selective', only letting Na^+ ions and water through it. Which ions are present in the positive electrode compartment but not in the negative electrode compartment?

c Copy and complete this ionic equation for the reaction at the positive electrode.

$$Cl^- \rightarrow Cl_2$$

d Copy and complete this ionic equation for the reaction at the negative electrode.

$$H^+ \rightarrow H_2$$

e Where do the hydrogen ions come from?

3.9 The noble gases

Key points

- Group 0 contains the unreactive noble gases.
- The Group shows trends in density and boiling points.
- The noble gases have many uses.

name	symbol	atomic number	neutrons in nucleus	percentage in dry air	density in g/cm³	boiling point in °C	date of discovery
Helium	He	2	2	0.0005	0.17	−269	1895
Neon	Ne	10	10	0.0018	0.83	−246	1898
Argon	Ar	18	22	0.93	1.7	−153	1894
Krypton	Kr	36	48	0.0001	3.5	−157	1898
Xenon	Xe	54	77	0.00001	5.5	−112	1998
Radon*	Rn	86	136	too little to detect			1900

*radioactive

1 Use the data in the table at the top of this page to work out the relative atomic mass for each of the noble gases by using the atomic number and the number of neutrons for each element. Put your results in a table with headings as shown:

name	atomic number	number of neutrons	relative atomic mass

2

a Use the data in the table at the top of this page to draw a bar graph to show the densities of the noble gases helium to xenon. Use it to estimate the density of the radioactive noble gas radon.

b Find the difference in boiling point between helium and xenon. Divide it to by four to get the 'average' difference. Use this to estimate the boiling point of radon.

c The actual boiling point is −62 °C. Suggest why this is higher than the estimated one. (Hint! Look at the difference in relative atomic masses.)

3 State a use for each of these gases:

a helium;   b neon;   c krypton.

─ IDEAS AND EVIDENCE ─

4 Using the data in the table at the top of this page write out the dates of discovery of the noble gases starting with the earliest. By each date put the name of the gas discovered and its percentage in dry air. Suggest a reason why the gases were discovered in this order.

5 From the data at the top of this page, work out the electron arrangement for atoms of helium, neon and argon.

The electron arrangement for:

krypton is (2,8,18,8)
xenon is (2,8,18,18,8) and
radon is (2,8,18,32,18,8).

a With reference to these arrangements:

i why is helium classified as a noble gas?

ii what is the more usual number of electrons in the outermost shell?

iii why is it to be expected that these gases are very unreactive?

b When elements combine using covalent bonds, what do they try to achieve in the outer shell of electrons?

c Compounds of xenon and fluorine have been made, e.g. XeF_2 and XeF_4.

What does this suggest about the electrons in the outer shells in these compounds?

d Assuming that radon is so radioactive that its compounds are too difficult to investigate, suggest why xenon is likely to be the least unreactive chemically.

e If you were researching for other elements with which xenon might react, which two other elements would you choose to investigate first. Give a reason.

3.10 Discovering the secrets of the atom

Key points

- It took many years to find out what atoms look like.
- Some important and famous scientists helped to make these discoveries.

---

1 Decide whether each of these statements is **true** or **false**.

a Atoms of the same element are all identical.

b Atoms of the same element all have the same atomic number.

c Atoms of the same element all have the same atomic mass.

d Atoms in the same period of the Periodic Table all have the same number of electrons in their outer shell.

e Atoms of the same element with different numbers of neutrons are called isotopes.

f A neutral atom has the same number of protons and electrons.

g An atom is changed into an ion by altering the number of protons in it.

h A neutral atom is one which does not react with acids or alkalis.

---

2 A radiographer is a person who takes and analyses X-ray photographs of patients. A radiographer normally wears a heavy apron made from lead. Why is this?

---

3 Chlorine can exist as two **isotopes**, $^{35}_{17}Cl$ and $^{37}_{17}Cl$.

75% of chlorine atoms are the lighter isotope and 25% are the heavier one.

a Explain what is meant by the term 'isotope'.

b What can be deduced from the two isotopic symbols with respect to:

  i the number of particles present

  ii the relative atomic mass of chlorine?

---

4 Molybdenum is a metal which can be used in motor vehicle oils to help overcome friction. It has seven different isotopes. The percentage of each is shown in the table. Work out the relative atomic mass of molybdenum.

mass number	percentage present
92	15.86
94	9.12
95	15.70
96	16.50
97	9.45
98	23.75
100	9.62

IDEAS AND EVIDENCE

5 In 1911, Rutherford's assistants Geiger and Marsden found that when alpha particles were aimed at thin gold sheets the alpha particles passed through them without making any holes. Some of the particles went straight ahead, others were deflected to one side and others bounced back.

Rutherford suggested three explanations of what happened to the various particles.

1. This alpha particle passes through the 'space' around the nucleus in a gold atom.

2. This alpha particle is deflected because the positive charges in the gold atom repel the positive charges on the alpha particle.

3. This alpha particle has approached a gold atom almost head on and has been repelled backwards.

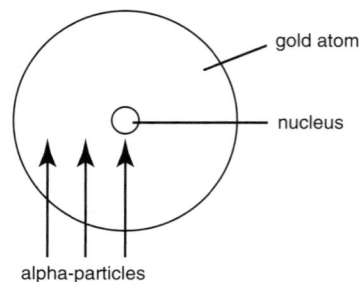

a Copy the diagram.

b Decide which of the explanations above fits which alpha particle in the diagram, and complete the diagram to show the path each particle might take. Label the alpha-particles 1, 2 or 3 to correspond to the explanations.

4.1 Following reaction progress

Key points

- We can find out how fast a reaction is going by measuring the disappearance of a reactant or the formation of a product.
- These measurements can be used to plot graphs.
- Finding the rate of a reaction also involves measuring time.

---

1 Pupils in a school investigated the rate of reaction of sandstone with hydrochloric acid. They had samples of sandstone from a local quarry. Sandstone is made of sand (silicon dioxide) which does not react with acid, stuck together with calcium carbonate. The calcium carbonate dissolves in the acid. The pupils measured the loss in mass during the reaction, using a balance connected to a computer, as shown in the diagram.

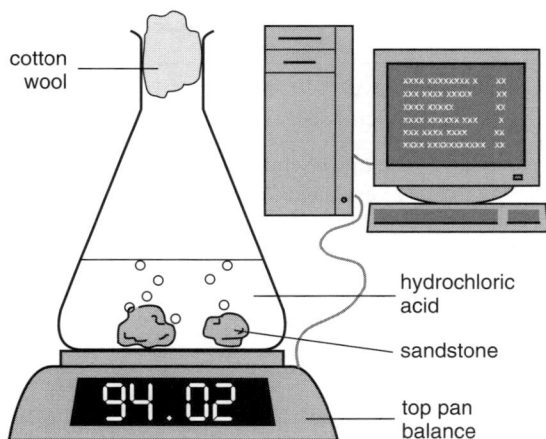

cotton wool
hydrochloric acid
sandstone
top pan balance
94.02

The computer printout gave this data.

time in minutes	mass lost in g
0	0
4	1.75
8	3.00
12	3.75
16	4.25
20	4.75
24	5.10
28	5.10
32	5.10

a Why does the flask lose mass during the reaction?

b Plot a graph of the results.

c What advantages are there in using a computer to collect the data?

d Calculate the rate of reaction:
  i during the first four minutes
  ii between 12 and 16 minutes
  iii between 28 and 32 minutes.

e How does the rate change during the reaction? Explain why this happens.

f At the end of the reaction, there was waste solid and solution left in the flask. List the names and chemical formulae of all of the compounds left in the flask (there are at least four).

IDEAS AND EVIDENCE

2 Science pupils were investigating the effects of acid rain on a local sandstone church. They planned to visit the church to collect evidence about where the damage was happening most quickly and why. They were not allowed to take samples of the stone, as this would damage the church. These are some of their ideas.

'We need to look at the stone outside.'

'I think we'll need to look at the stone inside as well.'

'We need to find out about the weather. How much rain is there and is it acidic?'

'What about which way the wind blows the rain? And which walls get most sunshine?'

'We could look at the gravestones too.'

Make a list of what evidence you think the pupils should look for. For each idea, say what you think they will see.

4.2 Faster and slower

Key points

- The rate of reaction is affected by change in concentration, temperature and the size of any solid pieces.

- Pressure has an effect on the rate of reactions involving gases.

1 In 1982 there was an explosion in a flour mill in the town of Metz in France. Huge blocks of concrete were thrown onto the motorway, 250 m away. The fine flour dust makes a fog in the factory. If even a small amount gets hot from a spark or a hot surface, it will start to burn and very quickly all the flour ignites and explodes.

Since the explosion safety measures have been introduced including...

- Dust proof doors which must be kept shut have been put into the factory.
- Workers must wear special shoes which do not cause friction against the floors.
- There are no naked flames allowed, no smoking and no hot surfaces. Even cooking and kettles are only allowed in certain, dust proof areas.

The workers find these safety rules difficult to keep.

Design a one-page leaflet to explain to workers why these rules are necessary. In your leaflet, use diagrams of the collision theory to show why fine flour dust can cause explosions.

2 List as many different ways of cooking potatoes as you can think of. Look in cookery books or ask members of your family for ideas.

a How long does each method take to cook the potato?

b Use ideas about rates of reaction and collision theory to explain why the different methods take different amounts of time.

3 Sam carried out an experiment to investigate the rate of reaction of copper(II) carbonate with hydrochloric acid, as shown in the diagram.

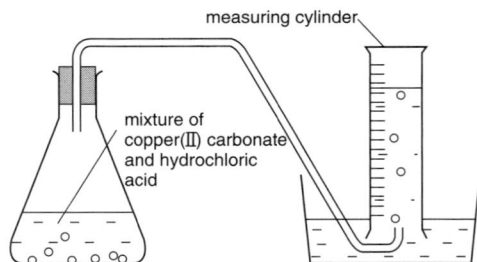

a What gas is made during the reaction?

b Sam carried out several experiments and plotted his results on a graph, as shown. However, he forgot to label most of the lines.

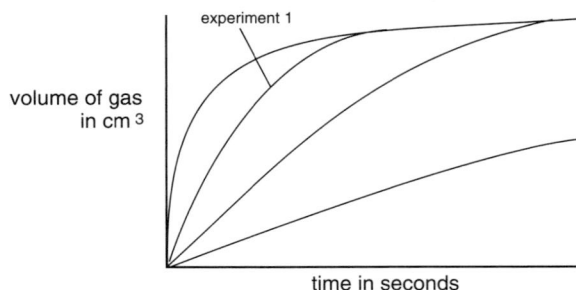

Experiment 1	Powdered copper(II) carbonate and 25 cm^3 acid
Experiment 2	Lumps of copper(II) carbonate and 25 cm^3 acid
Experiment 3	Powdered copper(II) carbonate and 25 cm^3 hot acid
Experiment 4	Lumps of copper(II) carbonate and 25 cm^3 diluted acid

Make a sketch copy of the graph and label the lines which show the results of experiments 2 to 4.

c Carbon dioxide dissolves slightly in water.

i What effect might this have on the experiment?

ii Suggest a way of carrying out this experiment avoiding this problem. You must use the same apparatus.

4.3 Catalysts

> ### Key points
>
> - A catalyst affects the rate of a reaction but is not used up.
> - Different reactions need different catalysts.

1 This diagram shows the structure of a catalytic converter in a car exhaust.

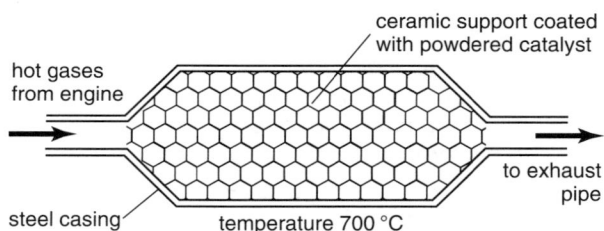

a List the reasons why the reactions in this converter are very fast.

b The rhodium/platinum catalyst is very expensive to buy, but works without needing to be replaced. Explain why.

These chemical reactions happen in the converter.

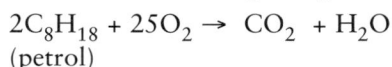

$$2CO + 2NO \rightarrow CO_2 + N_2$$
$$2C_8H_{18} + 25O_2 \rightarrow CO_2 + H_2O$$
(petrol)

c The right-hand sides of these equations are not balanced. Copy out the equations and balance them.

d These reactions are oxidation–reduction reactions. The main pollutants removed are carbon monoxide, nitrogen oxide and petrol.

  i Which of the elements in each of these pollutants has been oxidised?

  ii Which have been reduced?

  iii Explain how you can tell.

e Copy and complete this table to show all the gases going in and coming out of the converter.

gas in	environmental problem	gas out	environmental problem
NO	acid rain	N_2	none

f Some people believe that converters stop all pollution from cars. Explain whether or not you agree.

IDEAS AND EVIDENCE

2 Jo and Kim have been investigating the decomposition of hydrogen peroxide using catalysts. When the reaction occurs, the hydrogen peroxide produces oxygen.

$$2H_2O_2 \rightarrow 2H_2O + O_2$$

The catalysts they have tried are manganese(IV) oxide, MnO_2, and copper(II) oxide, CuO. Both are black powders.

Jo says she thinks that all black powders must be good catalysts. Kim thinks she is jumping to conclusions!

a What other factors do these two catalysts have in common (there are at least two)?

b What experiments will Jo and Kim need to do to find out what factor makes these compounds good catalysts? What other substances could they try? What evidence will they need to look for?

4.4 Enzymes

Key points

- Enzymes are biological catalysts produced by living things.
- Enzymes are proteins, sensitive to temperature and pH.
- Some industrial processes use enzymes.

1 A biochemist carried out some experiments on how the population of yeast changes when the conditions in the making of beer are changed.

The labels have been missed off the horizontal axis on each graph.

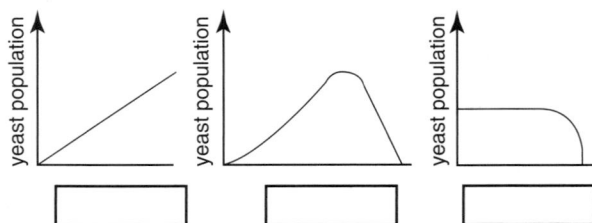

a Make sketch copies of these graphs. Write the following labels in the boxes on the correct graphs to show which condition is being changed in each case.

higher alcohol content	higher temperature	more food

b Use your graphs to explain why sugar is added to beer and fermented at 40°C. Why is it impossible to brew beer stronger than about 7% alcohol?

2 Biological washing powders contain the ingredients shown in this table.

ingredient	purpose
phosphates	softens hard water
detergent	cleans clothes
enzymes	dissolves food stains
bleach	makes white clothes whiter

a Use the information in the table and ideas about **enzymes** and **rates of reaction** to explain why:

i coloured clothes fade if they are washed in hot water regularly

ii the washing powder removes stains even in cooler washes at 40 °C

iii the washing machine programme for white cotton sheets uses water at 95 °C.

b Alex and Bobby were talking about how using washing powders affects the environment.

Washing powder harms the environment because of all the phosphates, bleaches and detergents running into the rivers.

No, biological washing powders save energy because you don't need to use very hot water. This is friendly to the environment.

Who do you think is right? What other information would you need to make a decision about whether using washing powders is harmful or beneficial to the environment?

5.1 Ions

Key points

- Atoms can form chemical bonds by transfer of electrons.
- This transfer of electrons forms charged particles called ions.
- Ions with a positive charge are formed by the loss of electrons from the outer shells of elements in Groups 1 and 2.
- Ions with a negative charge are formed by the gain of electrons into the outer shells of elements in Group 6 and 7.

1 Copy and complete this cross-word.

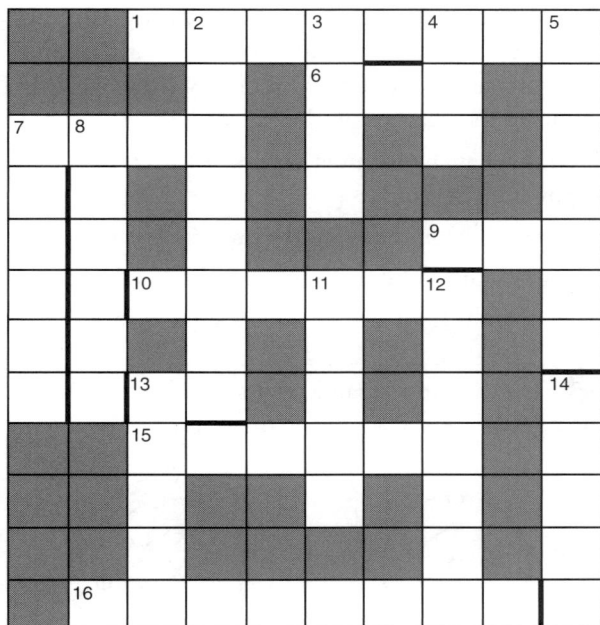

11. Number of charges on an aluminium ion (5)
12. This just adds mass to the nucleus (7)
13. In an ionic compound, the number of positive and negative charges is .... (5)
14. Electrons involved in making bonds are in the outer .... of an atom (5)

Across

1. Type of charge on a halide ion (8)
6. Number of charges on a calcium ion (3)
7. Metals .... away outer electrons to form ions (4)
9. Number of charges on an alkali metal ion (3)
10. Charged particle inside nucleus (6)
13. Transition metal symbol which has two positive charges on its ion (2)
15. Oxygen will ...... electrons to make its ion (6)
16. A gaseous element which needs one electron to complete its outer shell (8)

Down

2. Potassium loses this to make its ion (8)
3. Smallest part of an element (4)
4. Formed by gaining or losing electrons (3)
5. At least two are needed to form a compound (8)
7. Bromine turned into a bromide ion when it .... an electron (6)
8. This solid halogen needs one electron to form its ion (6)

2 Choose words from the list to complete these sentences. Words may be used once, more than once or not at all.

| atoms | electrons | ions | negative |
| positive | shell | removed | gained |

_____ can carry positive or negative charges. _____ charges on ions are caused by gaining _____ . Positive charges on ions occur when _____ are _____ . The electrons in the outer _____ of a metal can be transferred to a non-metal. The metal becomes a _____ ion and the non-metal a _____ ion. The number of charges carried depends on the number of _____ transferred.

3 a What trend is there in Group 1 in the ease by which atoms lose an electron?

   b What causes this trend?

4 a What trend is there in Group 7 in the ease by which atoms gain an electron?

   b What causes this trend?

5 Copy and complete this table about the particles present in these elements.

element	$^{7}_{3}Li^{+}$	$^{16}_{8}O^{2-}$	$^{24}_{12}Mg^{2+}$	$^{37}_{17}Cl^{-}$
protons				
neutrons				
electrons				

5.2 Ionic bonding (1)

Key points

- When elements in Group 1 or 2 react with elements in Group 6 or 7, electron transfer takes place.

- The ions that form attract each other forming ionic compounds.

1

a Which of the following elements will normally give positive ions and which will normally give negative ions? Make a list of each type.

b What general rule can you make to say what type of ion is produced?

c Are there any of these elements which do not normally form ions?

barium	calcium	carbon	chlorine
copper	fluorine	hydrogen	iodine
lithium	magnesium	nitrogen	oxygen
potassium	sodium	sulphur	zinc

2 Design a poster to show how atoms are converted into ions. Choose two suitable elements and show their electron arrangements as atoms and ions.

State on it the rule about what the atoms are attempting to reach when they change into ions.

3 Here are the 'dot and cross' diagrams for sodium and chlorine before and after the atoms are changed into ions. The ions attract each other to form sodium chloride.

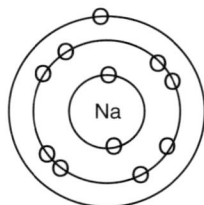
sodium atom

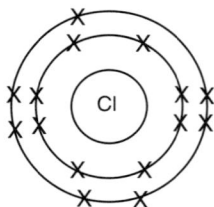
chlorine atom

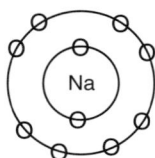
sodium ion

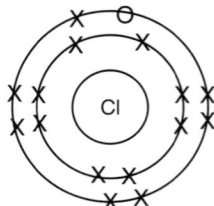
chloride ion

Draw similar diagrams to show how the following ionic compounds are made.

a potassium fluoride   d calcium fluoride

b calcium oxide   e lithium sulphide

c sodium oxide   f calcium chloride

4 Rubidium and caesium are in Group 1 of the Periodic Table. Bromide and iodine are in Group 7. The formula of sodium chloride is written as NaCl, ignoring the charges on the ions.

Predict what the formula will be for each of the following compounds.

a sodium bromide   d caesium oxide

b potassium iodide   e rubidium sulphide

c rubidium fluoride   f caesium chloride

5 The electron arrangements for element **Q** and element **X** are shown in the diagram.

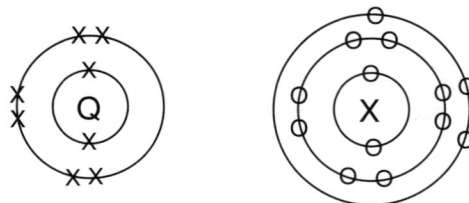

a How many electrons are gained when Q becomes an ion? Draw a diagram to show the electron arrangement in an ion of Q.

b How many electrons are lost when X becomes an ion? Draw a diagram to show the electron arrangement in an ion of X.

c What is the formula for the compound formed between Q and X?

6 Magnesium nitride is an ionic compound. Describe what electron transfers take place between magnesium and nitrogen and work out the formula for magnesium nitride.

7 Aluminium oxide is an ionic compound. Describe what electron transfers take place when aluminium oxide is formed and work out its formula.

5.3 Ionic bonding (2)

Key points

- There are strong forces of attraction between oppositely charged ions.
- These forces of attraction extend throughout the structure.
- In the solid state ions arrange themselves in a regular way to form a lattice.
- The whole of this lattice is called a giant structure.
- Ionic compounds have high melting and boiling points.

1 Copy and complete the following sentences by choosing words from the list.

electronic   electrostatic   ionic
magnetic   strong   weak

The attraction between oppositely charged ions is called _____ attraction. The attraction between oppositely charged ions is called an _____ bond. This type of bond is a very _____ bond.

2

a Water carries slight positive and negative charges. If sodium chloride crystals are added to it, they start to dissolve. Explain why this happens.

b Why are substances like candle wax or hydrogen gas virtually insoluble in water?

— IDEAS AND EVIDENCE —

3 These two tables show the melting points of some ionic compounds and the ionic radii of some ions.

compound	melting point in K
NaCl	1074
NaBr	1020
NaI	934
KCl	1043
KBr	1007
KI	954
RbCl	991
RbBr	966
RbI	920
MgO	3125
CaO	2887
SrO	2073

ion	ionic radius in nm
Na^+	0.102
K^+	0.138
Rb^+	0.149
Mg^{2+}	0.072
Ca^{2+}	0.100
Cs^{2+}	0.113
Cl^-	0.180
Br^-	0.195
I^-	0.215
O^{2-}	0.140
S^{2-}	0.180

a **i** Look at the ionic radii values Group 7 halide ions. What is the trend as Group 7 is descended from chloride to iodide?

 ii Now look at the melting points for the sodium halides. What is the trend descending the Group 7 sodium halides?

 iii Can you link these two trends into a general rule?

 iv Try your rule out on the rubidium halides. Does it work?

 v Does the rule work for the potassium halides?

b **i** Look at the values of the ionic radii for magnesium, calcium and strontium (Group 2). What is the trend as the Group is descended?

 ii Now look at the melting points of the Group 2 metal oxides. What is the trend descending the Group 2 metal oxides?

 iii Can you link these two trends into a general rule?

 i Look at the melting points of the metal chlorides in Group 1. What is the trend descending Group 1?

 ii What is the trend in the ionic radii descending the Group 1 metals?

 iii Does your rule from **b iii** apply to these values?

Na and Mg, K and Ca, Rb and Sr are adjacent pairs of metals in successive periods. Look at the ionic radius of the oxide ion, O^{2-}. From the general rules you have devised, can you explain why the melting points of the Group 2 metal oxides are appreciably higher than the Group 1 metal chlorides?

Predict whether the melting point of strontium sulphide (SrS) is going to be higher or lower than that of strontium oxide (SrO), giving your reasons.

5.4 **Covalent bonding (1)**

1 Unscramble the words in **bold** and copy and complete this paragraph.

Ionic bonds are usually formed by **aefnrrst** of electrons from a metal to a **onn-aelmt**. Covalent bonds usually occur between two non-metals and involve **aghinrs** electrons. Each of **otw** atoms gives one **ceelnort** to a **airp** which is then shared between the two.

ENO ADEHRS AIPR = ENO ACELNOTV BDNO.

Both atoms try to reach the electron arrangement of a **belno ags**.

2 Draw 'dot and cross' diagrams for the following substances in which all the bonds are single covalent bonds.

a hydrogen gas   c hydrogen chloride

b chlorine gas   d water

3 Covalent bonds can be shown as a straight line, as in the following diagrams. Each straight line represents a 'shared pair' of electrons.

Convert the following diagrams to 'dot and cross' diagrams. Be careful to put in any unused electrons too!

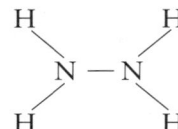

4 Draw 'dot and cross' diagrams for the following substances, some of which involve double or treble covalent bonds. You need only show the electrons in the outermost shells.

a i ethane, C_2H_6 iii oxygen, O_2
   ii carbon dioxide, CO_2 iv nitrogen, N_2

b Convert your answers in **a** to diagrams which show each covalent bond as a 'stick', as in question 3.

5 Convert the following diagrams of substances into 'dot and cross' diagrams to show the covalent bonds. You need only show the electrons in the outermost shells.

a ethene
$$\begin{array}{cc} H & H \\ | & | \\ C = C \\ | & | \\ H & H \end{array}$$

b methanol
$$\begin{array}{ccc} H & H \\ | & | \\ H - C - O - H \\ | & | \\ H & H \end{array}$$

c hydrazine
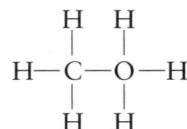

6 The formula for aluminium chloride is usually written as $AlCl_3$. There is strong evidence that it behaves as a covalent molecule.

a Convert the following diagram into a 'dot and cross' diagram to show the covalent bonds (show the outermost electrons only).

$$\begin{array}{c} Cl - Al - Cl \\ | \\ Cl \end{array}$$

b State two things which are unusual about this molecule.

7 Here are two important substances which are used to make polymers. Glycine is the smallest amino-acid, from which natural protein polymers can be made. 'Vinyl chloride' (or chloro-ethene) is the substance from which poly(vinyl chloride) is made (PVC).

Convert the following diagrams into 'dot and cross' diagrams to show the covalent bonds. (Show the outermost electrons only.)

a glycine
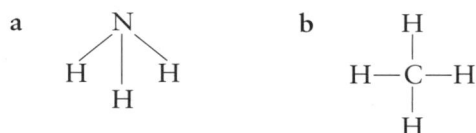

b vinyl chloride
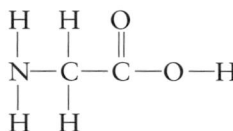

5.5 Covalent bonding (2)

Key points

H   Substances with covalent bonding are usually in the form of simple molecules.

H   Although the bonds inside the molecules themselves are strong, there are only very weak forces between the separate molecules.

H   Simple molecular compounds are said to have molecular structures.

H   Many substances with molecular structures are gases or liquids, though some are solids with low melting points.

1   In a test, Jane had to write some statements about covalent bonding. She scored five marks out of eight. Here are her eight statements. Which of them are incorrect and in what way?

a   A covalent compound contains bonds made by sharing pairs of electrons.

b   Covalent compounds are usually gases because the covalent bonds are strong bonds.

c   Covalent compounds usually have low melting points.

d   There are weak bonds between covalent molecules so the boiling points are usually low.

e   Covalent liquids have stronger bonds between their molecules than covalent solids.

f   Covalent gases have no attraction between molecules.

g   When a covalent liquid is cooled sufficiently, it freezes and becomes a giant lattice.

2   Design a poster to explain why methane in 'natural gas' is a covalent gaseous compound.

3   At room temperature:
- sodium bromide, NaBr, is a crystalline substance with a high melting point of 747 °C
- hydrogen bromide is a gas which boils at –67 °C.

Explain these two statements in terms of the different types of bonding involved.

4   This table shows the melting points and boiling points of some substances in °C.
(Room temperature = 25 °C.)

substance	melting point	boiling point
tin(IV) chloride	–33	114
potassium bromide	734	1435
propane	–190	–42
aluminium oxide	2072	2980
ethene (C_2H_4)	–169	–104
lithium fluoride	845	1340
decane ($C_{10}H_{22}$)	–30	174
eicosane ($C_{20}H_{42}$)	36	344

a   Which of these substances at room temperature:
  i   are gases
  ii   are liquids
  iii   are crystalline solids
  iv   is probably a waxy solid?

b   Which substances appear to be covalent substances? What is the evidence?

c   Which substances appear to be ionic substances? What is the evidence?

d   Which substance by its content might be expected to be ionic but appears to be covalent? Give your reason.

5   Here are the melting points and boiling points of some of the Group 4 chlorides in °C.

	CCl_4	$SiCl_4$	$GeCl_4$	$PbCl_4$
melting point	–23	–70	–33	–15
boiling point	77	58	16	105 explosive

a   Based on the information in the table, what sort of bonding is present inside these molecules? Give your reason.

b   Lead(II) chloride ($PbCl_2$) melts at 501 °C and boils at 950 °C. What does this suggest about the type of bonding in lead(II) chloride?

c   i   How many electrons are in the outer shell of all the Group 4 elements?
  ii   Suggest why the valency in $PbCl_4$ is **not** the same as that in $PbCl_2$.

6   Hydrogen chloride gas is a covalent substance, yet it dissolves in water. The resulting solution is hydrochloric acid, which readily conducts electricity.

a   Why will hydrogen chloride gas not conduct electricity?

b   Explain what happens when hydrogen chloride gas is mixed with water.

c   Why will hydrochloric acid conduct electricity?

5.6 **Carbon**

Key points

H   Atoms that share electrons by covalent bonding can sometimes form giant structures.

H   Examples include graphite and diamond, which are both forms of the element carbon.

H   Substances that have a giant lattice of covalent bonds have high melting points and high boiling points.

H   Recently chemists discovered that carbon atoms could also form molecules.

1   The atomic number of carbon is 6.

a   What is the electron arrangement in carbon?

b   What is the largest number of electrons that can be used for bonding in a carbon atom?

c   What type of bonding would you expect carbon to have? Give a reason for your answer.

2   Ann's zip in her skirt became stiff to move. She rubbed it gently with a soft pencil to help it to move more easily. Why does this method work?

Why is a pencil better than oil for this job?

3   Why might it be better to use graphite rather than oil to lubricate the moving parts of machinery used at high temperature?

4   Here is a diagram of the carbon atoms in diamond.

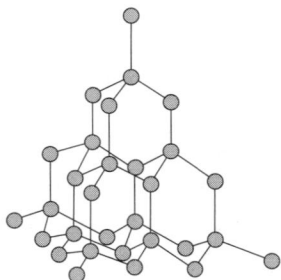

a   How many electrons per atom of carbon are used to form bonds to other carbon atoms in diamond?

b   Sketch the basic 'unit' which is repeated in diamond. (This will involve five atoms.) What word is used to describe this shape?

c   Diamond is the hardest known naturally occurring substance. Why is it so hard?

d   What words are used to classify a crystalline structure like diamond?

e   Why does diamond have such a high melting point (3550 °C)?

5   Here is a diagram of the carbon atoms in graphite.

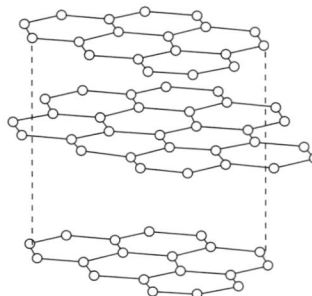

a   How many electrons per atom of carbon are used to form bonds to other carbon atoms in graphite?

b   Sketch the basic 'unit' which is repeated in graphite? (This will involve six atoms.) What word is used to describe this shape?

c   How many carbon atoms are linked to each other carbon atom? What is the 'bond angle' between carbon atoms?

d   Graphite has a 'layer' structure. Each layer is 2.5 times further apart than the carbon atoms in any one layer. What does this mean about the strength of the bonds **between** adjacent layers?

e   Suggest what is used to hold these layers together.

f   Graphite can be used as a lubricant. Explain why.

6   Explain each of the following statements.

a   Graphite can conduct electricity but diamond does not.

b   Diamond is used in glass-cutters but graphite is not.

c   Graphite is mixed with clay to make the 'lead' in pencils. The 'hardness' of the pencil depends on the relative amounts of graphite and clay in the mixture.

d   Diamond is used in drills for boring through rocks.

e   Graphite fibres can reinforce tennis racket frames.

5.7 Formula calculations (1)

Key points

- The relative formula mass of a substance can be calculated from its formula.
- The percentage of each element in a substance can be calculated from its formula.
- Masses of reacting substances can be calculated from balanced equations.
- The formula of a compound can be calculated from the masses of substances that combine to make it.

relative atomic masses	
Ag	108
Al	27
C	12
Ca	40
Cl	35.5
Cu	64
Fe	56
Mg	24
N	14
Na	23
O	16
P	31
Pb	207
S	32
Zn	65

1 How much copper is released when 8 g of copper(II) oxide is completely reduced by heating it in hydrogen? The equation for the reaction is:

$$CuO + H_2 \rightarrow Cu + H_2O$$

2 How much ammonium chloride is made when 3.4 g of ammonia react with excess hydrogen chloride? The equation for the reaction is:

$$NH_3 + HCl \rightarrow NH_4Cl$$

3 How much carbon dioxide is set free when 50 g of calcium carbonate react completely with hydrochloric acid?

$$CaCO_3 + 2HCl \rightarrow CaCl_2 + H_2O + CO_2$$

4 How much sodium hydroxide is needed to neutralise 12.6 g of nitric acid?

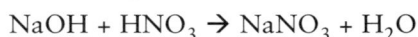

$$NaOH + HNO_3 \rightarrow NaNO_3 + H_2O$$

5 Find the simplest formulae of the compounds made from these combinations of elements from their percentage composition by mass.

a Cu 80%, O 20%   b Fe 63.6%, S 36.4%

c H 20%, C 80%   d P 43.7%, O 56.3%

6 Find the relative formula mass of the following substances.

a magnesium oxide, MgO

b sodium hydroxide, $NaOH$

c nitric acid, HNO_3

d aluminium oxide, Al_2O_3

e zinc carbonate, $ZnCO_3$

f ammonium sulphate, $(NH_4)_2SO_4$

g lead(II) nitrate, $Pb(NO_3)_2$

h iron(II) hydroxide, $Fe(OH)_2$

i copper(II) hydroxide $Cu(OH)_2$

7 Find the percentage of the named element in each case.

a calcium in calcium carbonate, $CaCO_3$

b copper in copper(II) oxide, CuO

c magnesium in magnesium oxide, MgO

d oxygen in nitrogen dioxide, NO_2

e iron in iron(III) hydroxide, $Fe(OH)_3$

f nitrogen in ammonium nitrate, NH_4NO_3

g aluminium in aluminium sulphate, $Al_2(SO_4)_3$

h water in hydrated copper(II) sulphate crystals, $CuSO_4.5H_2O$

8 How much iron(II) hydroxide can be formed when excess iron(II) sulphate solution is added to a solution containing 16 g of sodium hydroxide? The equation for the reaction is:

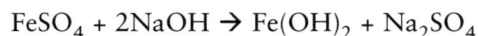

$$FeSO_4 + 2NaOH \rightarrow Fe(OH)_2 + Na_2SO_4$$

Continued ▶

5.7 Formula calculations (2)

9 A compound contains 63.5 g silver, 8.2 g nitrogen and 28.2 g oxygen. What is its simplest formula?

10 Some limestone is 80% pure. How much quicklime (calcium oxide) can be made when 500 tonnes of limestone is heated in a limekiln? The equation for the reaction is:

$$CaCO_3 \rightarrow CaO + CO_2$$

11 1400 tonnes of nitrogen are completely converted into ammonia. The ammonia is then absorbed by sulphuric acid to make ammonium sulphate fertiliser. What is the theoretical yield of this fertiliser?

$$N_2 + 3H_2 \rightarrow 2NH_3$$
$$2NH_3 + H_2SO_4 \rightarrow (NH_4)_2SO_4$$

12 A hydrocarbon contains 7.7 % hydrogen and 92.3% carbon. Its formula mass is known to be about 80. Find its accurate formula mass.

13 Find the simplest formula of a compound which contains 7 g of iron and 3 g of oxygen.

14 A zinc compound contains 22.7 g zinc, 11.1 g sulphur, 22.2 g oxygen and 44 g of water of crystallisation. Work out its simplest formula.

15 The general formula of organic acids is $C_nH_{2n+1}CO_2H$. One of these acids contains 40.0% carbon, 6.7% hydrogen and 53.3% oxygen.

a What is its simplest formula?

b Which acid is it?

16 A hydrocarbon contains 14.3% hydrogen and 85.7% carbon. When it burns completely, it produces 3 moles of carbon dioxide from every mole of the hydrocarbon. When the hydrocarbon is shaken with orange bromine water, the colour immediately disappears.

a Find the simplest formula of the hydrocarbon.

b Which hydrocarbon is it?

5.8 Energy changes

Key points

H   Covalent bonds between different atoms require particular amounts of energy to break them.

H   This is called the bond energy of that bond.

H   Breaking of bonds requires energy and is endothermic.

H   Making bonds releases energy and is exothermic.

H   Overall energy changes for a reaction can be calculated by considering bonds broken in the reactants and formed in products.

H   Energy changes in reactions can be represented by energy level diagrams.

1 a Energy is needed to break covalent bonds. What name is given to this sort of energy change?

   b When new bonds are formed, energy is released. What name is given to this sort of energy change?

2 The energy needed to break or make a bond is called the 'bond energy'. Use this table of bond energies to answer the questions that follow.

bond	average bond energy in kJ	bond	average bond energy in kJ
H–H	436	O=O	496
H–Cl	431	O–H	463
H–Br	366	Cl–Cl	242
C–H	412	Br–Br	193
C–C	348	Si–Si	226
C–O	358	N≡N	944
C=O	743	N–H	391
C–Cl	346		

a Why does the table use 'average' bond energies?

b Which bond is the easiest to break?

c Suggest why the value for C=O is more than the value for C — C.

d There are many stable long-chain carbon compounds containing C — C bonds. There are far fewer compounds containing Si — Si bonds. Suggest why.

e Nitrogen gas is very unreactive. Suggest why this is so.

3 Hydrogen and bromine gases react together to form hydrogen bromide, as in the equation:

$$H_2 + Br_2 \rightarrow 2HBr$$

a How much energy is needed to break the bonds in one formula mass of hydrogen molecules and one formula mass of bromine molecules?

b How much energy is given out when two formula masses of hydrogen bromide are made?

c State with reference to your answers whether the overall reaction is endothermic or exothermic.

4 Methane can react with chlorine to produce chloromethane and hydrogen chloride as in the equation:

$$CH_4 + Cl_2 \rightarrow CH_3Cl + HCl$$

a How much energy is needed to break one C—H formula mass of bonds?

b How much energy is needed to break the bonds in one formula mass of chlorine molecules?

c How much energy is given out when one formula mass of C—Cl bonds is made?

d How much energy is given out when one formula mass of H—Cl bonds is made?

e State with reference to your answers whether the overall reaction is endothermic or exothermic.

f Sketch the energy changes in this reaction on an energy level diagram.

IDEAS AND EVIDENCE

5 Ammonia is made in the reversible Haber process as shown in the equation:

$$N_2 + 3H_2 \rightleftharpoons 2NH_3$$

a Work out how much energy is needed to break all the bonds in the formula masses of nitrogen and hydrogen.

b Work out the energy given out in making two formula masses of ammonia.

c From your results, decide in which direction the reaction is exothermic.

d The manufacturer has to decide whether to try to speed up the reaction by running the process at a higher temperature. In the light of your results, what else must be taken into account?

6.1 Crude oil

Key points

- Crude oil is a mixture of many substances.
- Most of the substances in crude oil are hydrocarbons.

- Fractional distillation is used to separate the hydrocarbons into fractions, each with a different boiling point range.

---

1 Crude oil can be separated in the laboratory by soaking it onto mineral wool and heating it using the apparatus shown in the diagram.

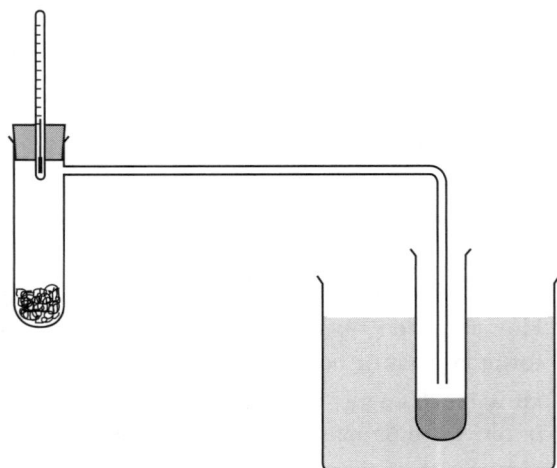

a Copy the diagram and label it with these labels.

mineral wool	delivery tube
thermometer	heat
water bath	fraction

b Explain why these parts of the apparatus are important:

i the thermometer
ii the mineral wool
iii the water bath.

c Four fractions with different boiling point ranges were collected as shown in the table.

fraction	boiling point range in °C
1	30–80
2	80–115
3	115–190
4	190–300

i Which fractions are liquids at 100°C?
ii Which fraction has the largest molecules?
iii Which fraction would come out of the top of a fractionating tower?

---

2 This diagram shows a fractionating tower which breaks crude oil into fractions in an oil refinery.

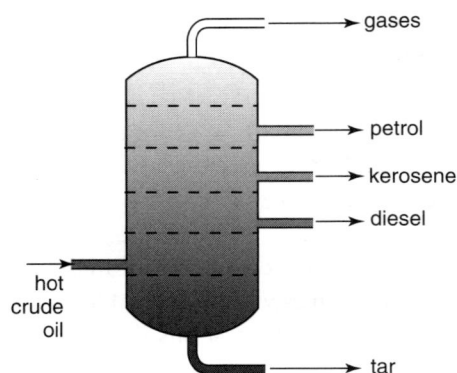

a Explain what happens to a molecule of octane, C_8H_{18}, in the fractionating tower. Octane leaves the tower as part of the petrol fraction. You need to use these words in your explanation.

enters	crude oil	petrol	heated
evaporate	cool	condense	fraction
liquid	gas	mixture	

b Even though the fuels in the fractionating tower get very hot, they do not burn. Explain why.

c Petrol and diesel are separated because they have different boiling points. Which compound has the higher boiling point? Explain why the difference in boiling points causes the two fuels to come out of the tower in different places.

d Complete the symbol equation for the cracking of octane:
$$C_{18}H_{18} \rightarrow C_2H_4 +$$

6.2 Fuels

Key points

- The hydrocarbons obtained from crude oil have many uses.
- One of these is their use as fuels in combustion reactions.

- The products of this combustion of hydrocarbons may be harmful to the environment or even toxic.

1 'Natural gas' used in houses is mainly methane. When methane burns completely it produces carbon dioxide and water.

$$CH_4 + 2O_2 \rightarrow CO_2 + 2H_2O$$

From looking at the equation, we can see that 1 molecule of methane needs 2 molecules of oxygen to burn completely.

It follows that …
1 dm³ of methane needs **2 dm³ of oxygen**
to burn completely.

a Remembering that about 20% of air is oxygen, what volume of **air** would be needed to completely burn 1 dm³ of methane?

b If this amount of air is not available, the methane does not burn completely. What gas will be formed? Why is this very hazardous in the home?

c If you have a central heating boiler or gas fire in your home, make a survey of the room. How does air enter the room? What limits the amount of air entering the room?

d The death rate from inhaling the gases from incomplete combustion has risen since double glazing became popular. Explain why.

2 Propane is sold as bottled gas for caravans.

a Write a symbol equation for the complete combustion of propane, C_3H_8.

b What volume of air is needed to completely burn 1 dm³ of propane? (Use the beginning of question 1 to help you).

c Why does propane need more air than methane to burn completely?

d Cookers for caravans using propane have to be adapted. If ordinary cookers are used, toxic gases can form. Explain why.

3 The table shows some information about the energy released when some hydrocarbons burn.

name	formula	energy released in kJ
methane	CH_4	890
ethane	C_2H_6	1560
propane	C_3H_8	2220
butane	C_4H_{10}	2880
pentane	C_5H_{12}	–
hexane	C_6H_{14}	4200

a Plot a graph of **energy released** against **number of carbon atoms,** for the hydrocarbons in the table.

b Use your graph to predict the energy released when pentane burns.

c What pattern links the number of carbon atoms to the amount of energy released on burning?

d The larger hydrocarbons tend to burn with smoky flames. This is because they often produce carbon rather than carbon dioxide.

Write a symbol equation to show:

　i pentane burning to make carbon and water
　ii pentane burning completely.

e Look at the two equations. Why do you think the larger hydrocarbons burn with smoky flames?

f Write balanced symbol equations for the burning of a hydrocarbon C_xH_y in

　i a plentiful supply of air
　ii a limited supply of air when carbon monoxide is formed.

6.3 Hydrocarbons

Key points

- Hydrocarbons can be put into families that have similar structures and similar chemical properties.

- Two of these families are called alkanes and alkenes.
- Hydrocarbons in the same family have the same general formula.

1 **a** What is meant by the term hydrocarbon?
Ethane is a saturated hydrocarbon.

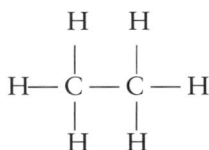

$$H-\underset{\underset{H}{|}}{\overset{\overset{H}{|}}{C}}-\underset{\underset{H}{|}}{\overset{\overset{H}{|}}{C}}-H$$

b What is meant by saturated?

c What is the molecular formula of ethane?

2 Propanol is a solvent that was used for dry cleaning clothes. This is the displayed structure of propanol.

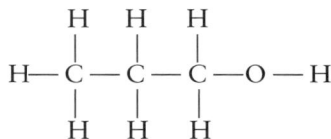

$$H-\underset{\underset{H}{|}}{\overset{\overset{H}{|}}{C}}-\underset{\underset{H}{|}}{\overset{\overset{H}{|}}{C}}-\underset{\underset{H}{|}}{\overset{\overset{H}{|}}{C}}-O-H$$

a Write the molecular formula for propanol.

b Would you expect propanol to react with bromine water? Explain your reasoning.

c Propanol is very flammable and is harmful to inhale. What safety precautions would the workers in the dry cleaners need to take when they used propanol?

d When the dry cleaning solvent gets dirty, the propanol can be recycled by distilling it and leaving behind the dirt. The diagram shows the apparatus that can be used to distil propanol.

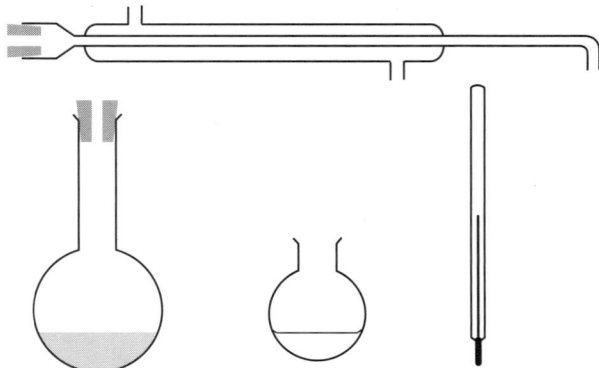

Draw the apparatus fully set up to distil propanol. Include these labels on your diagram.

condenser	water in	water out
heat	thermometer	ice bath

Propanol is a member of a family called the alcohols. The table shows some other members of the alcohol family.

name	formula
ethanol	
propanol	C_3H_7OH
butanol	C_4H_9OH

e Copy the table and fill in the formula for ethanol.

f Predict which of these alcohols:

  i has the highest boiling point
  ii is the most flammable.

3 'CFC's are chemicals that were used in aerosols. They contain chlorine atoms which damage the ozone layer.

A CFC has the formula CF_2Cl_2. It is a saturated compound with a similar structure to methane.

a What does **'saturated'** mean?

b Draw the displayed formula of CF_2Cl_2.

c This is the displayed formula for $C_2F_2Cl_2$.

$$\underset{\underset{F}{|}}{\overset{\overset{F}{|}}{C}}=\underset{\underset{Cl}{|}}{\overset{\overset{Cl}{|}}{C}}$$

Explain how you could use bromine water to distinguish between $C_2F_2Cl_2$ and CF_2Cl_2.

Another compound has the formula CF_2H_2.

d Draw the displayed formula for CF_2H_2.

e Would you expect CF_2H_2 to damage the ozone layer? Explain your reasoning.

6.4 Cracking

Key points

- The fractions that are obtained from crude oil are not in equal demand from consumers.

- Smaller hydrocarbons are generally in greater demand than larger ones.
- Cracking breaks down larger hydrocarbons into smaller ones.

1 This apparatus can be used in the laboratory to crack solid petroleum jelly.

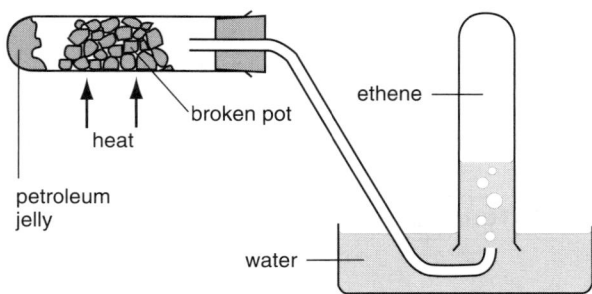

a What evidence is there that larger molecules have been broken down to make smaller molecules?

b This process involves both **thermal cracking** and **catalytic cracking**. Explain what these terms mean.

c One of the products of the reaction is ethene, an unsaturated alkene. The formula for ethene is C_2H_4. Write an equation for the reaction of ethene with bromine. Use **displayed formulae**.

d What would you **see** if bromine water was shaken with the test tube of ethene gas?

e Explain why a thin oily layer is found on the water in the trough at the end of the experiment.

2 A letter of complaint was published in a newspaper about a local oil refinery.

Dear Editor,

Why is NS Oil buying oil from outside Europe? Why does the company not buy all their oil from our own British suppliers in the North Sea? Support our own country's industry, that's what I say.

Yours,

Angry Oil Consumer (Aberbourne)

This bar chart shows a comparison of demand and supply for the fractions of oil from the North Sea.

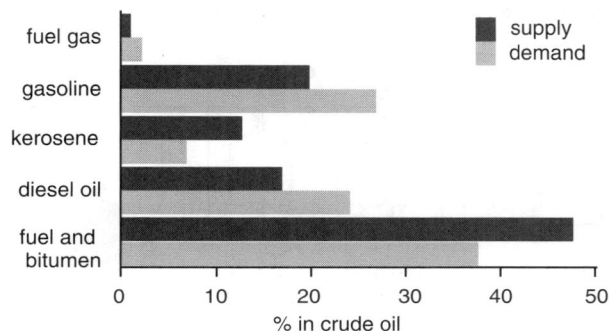

This table shows information about the percentage composition of North Sea and imported crude oil.

fraction	percentage of North Sea oil	percentage of imported oil
gas	2	2
gasoline	20	12
kerosene	13	16
diesel	17	20
fuel oil and bitumen	48	50

Suppose you work as a buyer for NS Oil. Write a letter to the newspaper to explain:

a why NS Oil buys both North Sea and imported oil

b why it is important to make demand meet supply for both the environment and for the company's profits

c what chemical processes NS Oil already uses to change North Sea oil to meet demand to save buying oil from overseas.

6.5 Polymers

Key points

- Under suitable conditions alkene molecules join up with themselves to produce long chains of carbon atoms.
- The small alkene molecules that do this are called monomers.

- The long chain molecules that form are called polymers.
- The structure of a polymer is determined by the structure of the monomer.

1 Poly(propene) is a polymer used to make plastic packaging. It is a **thermoplastic**, and so it can be moulded by melting it and blowing it into moulds.

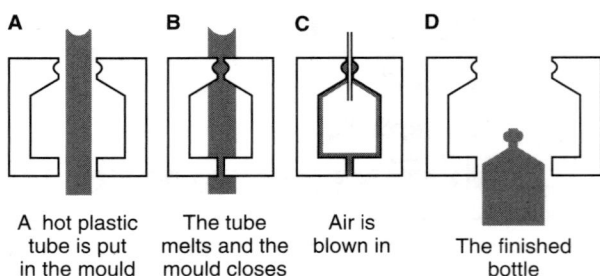

A A hot plastic tube is put in the mould

B The tube melts and the mould closes

C Air is blown in

D The finished bottle

a Use ideas about particles in solids and liquids to describe what happens to the poly(propene) chains when they melt (diagram B).

b This is the diplayed formula of poly(propene).

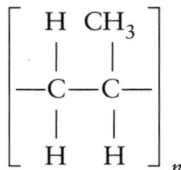

$$\left[\begin{array}{c} H\ CH_3 \\ |\quad | \\ -C-C- \\ |\quad | \\ H\quad H \end{array}\right]_n$$

Draw the displayed formula of the monomer, propene.

c Explain, using ideas about sizes of molecules, why polymers are usually solids but monomers are usually gases.

d The poly(propene) chains have an average molecular mass of 210 000.

   i Explain why this is an average.

   ii How many monomer molecules are there in an average poly(propene) molecule?

2 This is a flow chart for the manufacture of poly(ethene) from crude oil.

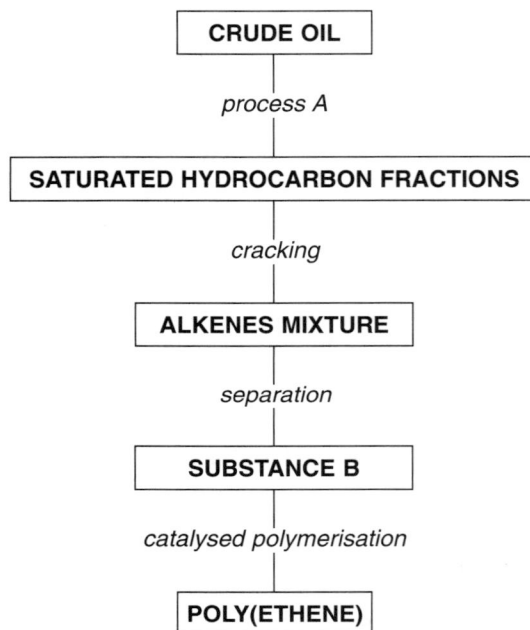

CRUDE OIL

process A

SATURATED HYDROCARBON FRACTIONS

cracking

ALKENES MIXTURE

separation

SUBSTANCE B

catalysed polymerisation

POLY(ETHENE)

a Copy and complete the flow chart by filling in the name of process A and substance B.

b Make a list of all the costs involved at each stage of the manufacture. Which processes use a lot of fuel (have a *high energy demand*)?

c Explain why using a catalyst during polymerisation reduces the energy demand for that part of the process.

6.6 Using polymers

Key points

- Polymers have many different uses.
- The use that a particular polymer has depends directly on the properties of that polymer.

- Scientists now try to make new polymers to fit particular needs.

1 This table shows the various components of household rubbish.

paper and board	35%
food and garden waste	25%
plastic	6%
glass	8%
metal	6%
other	20%

a What percentage of the rubbish will have rotted away after 50 years?

b Why do you think most recycling schemes are for glass, metal and paper?

2 Some types of poly(ethene) are **biodegradable** (can be broken down by bacteria). Poly(ethene) chains up to a molecular mass of 4800 are biodegradable. This is the structural formula of the repeating unit in poly(ethene).

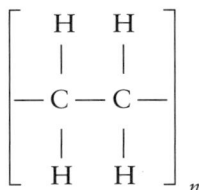

$$\begin{bmatrix} \begin{matrix} H & H \\ | & | \\ -C & -C- \\ | & | \\ H & H \end{matrix} \end{bmatrix}_n$$

a What is the molecular mass of a single repeating unit of poly(ethene)?

b How many repeating units are in a polymer chain of mass 4800?

Most poly(ethene) used today has much bigger chains with masses over 100 000. Short chain poly(ethene) is weaker and melts easily.

c Use ideas about lengths of polymer chains to explain why short chain poly(ethene) is weak and melts easily.

d Biodegradable plastics are used for low quality goods like plastic carrier bags but are not used for higher quality goods such as washing up bowls. Suggest why.

This graph shows how the amount of chlorine in the polymer plastic affects whether bacteria can grow on it and break it down.

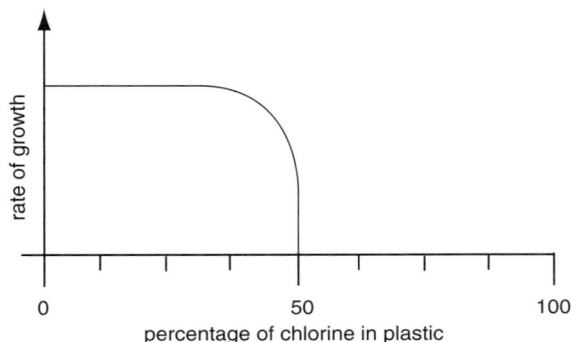

This is the structural formula of the repeating unit in PVC.

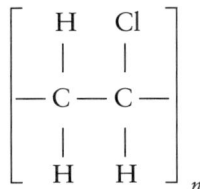

$$\begin{bmatrix} \begin{matrix} H & Cl \\ | & | \\ -C & -C- \\ | & | \\ H & H \end{matrix} \end{bmatrix}_n$$

e What is the molecular mass of the repeating unit in PVC?

f Calculate the percentage of chlorine in the repeating unit.

g Would you expect PVC to biodegrade? Explain your answer.

h Electrical wiring in houses used to be coated in rubber. New wiring is coated with PVC. Explain why it is worth paying to have rubber coated wiring replaced with PVC coated wiring in your house.

i When PVC burns, it can produce a gas that is very acidic. What is the name of this gas?

6.7 The oil industry

Key points

- The oil industry is most important for meeting the needs of today's society.
- A wide variety of scientists are needed in the oil industry.

- The potential environmental problems from the extraction, transport and refining of oil have to be addressed as does the disposal of oil-related products.

1 Crude oil can be used as a fuel or as a source of chemicals. This table shows the final uses of 10 barrels of crude oil.

final use	number of barrels
petrol for cars	3.0
central heating for houses	2.5
fuel for industry	1.5
making electricity	1.3
fuel for trains, aeroplanes and ships	0.7
making chemicals	1.0
total	10

a Make a bar chart showing this information.

b What percentage of oil is used as fuel?

c A group of students were planning to write a cartoon strip for the school magazine about how important it is to save oil supplies. Here are some of their views:

'We don't need to worry yet about finding alternative fuels. Oil won't run out for at least another 100 years.'

'We need to find alternative fuels now because it is such a waste to burn oil. We need to save it to make plastics, synthetic fibres, paints, detergents … I can't imagine life without shampoo!'

'My mum says alternative fuels will be too expensive anyway. Our bills are high enough as it is. Dad says there's no way he would have one of those windmill generators making a noise in the back garden all night.'

Use these ideas to help you write a science fiction strip cartoon for the school magazine. Show what life will be like if we have to go without the chemicals and fuels we get from crude oil.

2 A company called Search Oil have been test drilling for oil. They have found a large oil field underground near the villages of Sutland and Grillister.

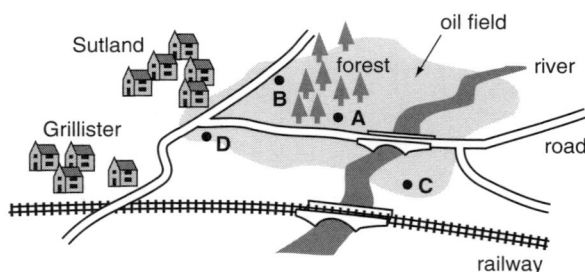

The oil is nearest the surface at point B on the map.

a Give reasons why the oil company would prefer to drill where oil is near the surface.

b The local people object to drilling at this site. Which site do you think would be the best choice for drilling? Explain your reasons.

c Local people are objecting to drilling because they are worried about:

- noise from the drilling and lorries
- heavy traffic through the villages
- the drilling will cause an eyesore
- the land will being permanently spoiled for wildlife, even after drilling is finished.

Suppose you work for Search Oil. What could the company do to address these problems so that local people did not object to the drilling?

d As an employee of Search Oil you are asked to write a piece for the local paper to inform the population of the plan. You should try to be as positive as possible about the project. You have a maximum of 250 words.

7.1 Air

Key points

- The present atmosphere has been much the same for the past 200 million years.
- Earth's atmosphere was probably formed about 4 thousand million years ago by volcanic activity.

- A pure sample of air in today's atmosphere contains about 80% nitrogen and 20% oxygen.

IDEAS AND EVIDENCE

1 Jo and Alex are investigating the amount of oxygen in air. They find the experiment shown below in a text book.

The text book says that when the candle uses the oxygen for burning, the water will rise 1/5 of the way up the jar, proving that air is 20% oxygen.

Jo and Alex try out the experiment, and also do some other research. They find out that:

- the water does rise 1/5 of the way up the jar, as the book says
- air expands when it gets hot and contracts when it is cold
- carbon dioxide dissolves easily in water
- carbon dioxide stops candles burning, even when there is oxygen left in the air.

Write an **evaluation** of this experiment. Is it a **valid** way of finding out the amount of oxygen in air? Why do you think that the value it gives is very close to the 'true' value of 20% oxygen?

2 In the eighteenth century, Joseph Priestley carried out experiments to make 'active air' from mercury calx. We now know that 'active air' is oxygen. He set up his experiment like this.

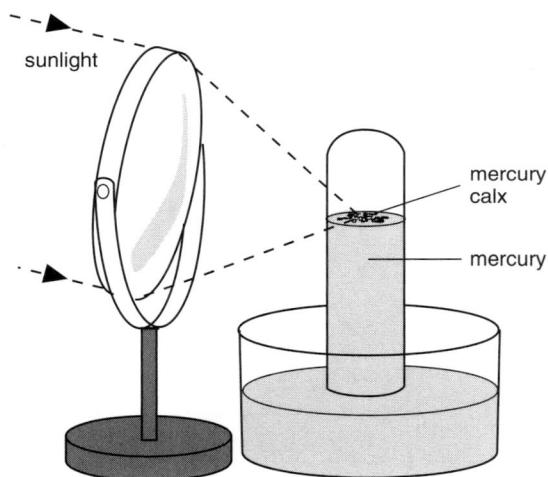

When the 'mercury calx' became hot, it made 'active air' (oxygen) and mercury.

a What compound must have been in 'mercury calx'?

b Draw some apparatus that you could use in the school laboratory to heat mercury calx and collect oxygen. What differences are there between your apparatus and Priestley's? Why are they so different?

c Priestley called oxygen 'active air' and called nitrogen 'inactive air'. What experiments do you think he carried out to believe that oxygen was 'active' and nitrogen was 'inactive'?

d Imagine that you are Joseph Priestley. Write a short script for a lecture to be given to your fellow scientists. Explain your experiments and what you have found out about 'active' and 'inactive' air.

7.2 The atmosphere

Key points

- The composition of Earth's early atmosphere slowly changed over millions of years.
- Cooling of the Earth's surface allowed steam to condense to water and this allowed the oceans to form.
- Evolution of photosynthesising organisms increased the amount of oxygen.

- Photosynthesis, the formation of fossil fuels and solution in the oceans decreased the amount of carbon dioxide.
- Ammonia was removed by bacteria and also by reaction with oxygen. This resulted in the formation of nitrogen.

1 This table shows how the composition of the atmosphere has changed since the Earth was formed.

millions of years ago	carbon dioxide %	gas X %	oxygen %
4500	90	10	0
4000	40	30	0
3500	20	40	trace
3000	15	55	1
2500	10	60	5
2000	7	80	10
1500	5	75	18
1000	2	77	20
500	1	77	21
0	trace	78	21

a Draw a graph to show how the amounts of the three gases have changed over time.

b What is the name of 'Gas X'? Explain how you can tell what this gas is.

c Mark the letters **A** and **B** on the time axis on your graph to show when the following events happened.

A first plants evolved, photosynthesis begins
B land animals evolved, respiration begins on land

The first oceans formed 4000 million years ago.

d Why did this cause the amount of atmospheric carbon dioxide to fall?

e When sea water is boiled, the air given off contains 33% oxygen and 67% nitrogen. What does this tell you about the solubilities of these gases in water? Why is this vital to life on Earth?

2 The table below shows information about the gases which come from an active volcano in Hawaii. Scientists think our early atmosphere came from similar volcanoes and so contained similar gases.

gas	% in volcanic gases	% in Earth's atmosphere today
nitrogen	5	78
oxygen	0	21
carbon dioxide	12	0.03
water vapour	74	<1
sulphur dioxide	9	trace

a Draw a comparison bar chart to show the amounts of each gas in our atmosphere 4000 million years ago compared to today (use a spreadsheet, if you have access to one).

b The water vapour condensed as the Earth cooled. How did this change the appearance of the Earth?

c Scientists think there was an earlier atmosphere of hydrogen and helium, but this atmosphere was lost. Look up the atomic masses of these gases on the Periodic Table. Why do you think hydrogen and helium left the Earth, but the other volcanic gases did not?

d Explain how and why the amounts of oxygen and carbon dioxide have changed over time.

7.3 The oceans

Key points

- When the Earth formed it was too hot for water to be present on the surface for hundreds of millions of years.
- When the temperature became low enough for the water to condense, the oceans formed.
- Water is a good solvent and dissolved some of the rocks it was in contact with.
- Over millions of years the mineral composition of the ocean has become constant.

---

1 This table shows some information about the ions found in sea water.

name	formula	percentage by mass in sea water
chloride		55
	Na^+	31
	SO_4^{2-}	8
magnesium		4
	Ca^{2+}	1.5
other ions	—	

a Copy and complete the table. Use the Periodic Table to help you.

b Draw a large diagram to show how ions enter the sea from land and underwater volcanoes. Include these labels on your diagram:

- Compounds containing sodium, calcium and magnesium ions are leached from the soil.
- Rivers carry ions in solution to the sea.
- Water from undersea volcanoes contains dissolved chlorine, bromine and sulphates.
- Very old rocks on land are weathered by rain and rivers.

c The sea also contains carbonate ions. These do not come from the land or volcanoes. Explain where they come from. Add the information to your diagram.

d Write a story or draw a flow diagram about an ion of calcium. Show how it came from a volcano 3000 million years ago, and travelled to form limestone on the sea floor. Include these words in your account:

| igneous | weathered | eroded |
| deposited | precipitate | sedimentary |

2 'Mineral water' comes from streams and rivers and contains dissolved ions. River water containing dissolved ions is a major source of ions in the sea. This information shows the contents of sea water compared to the contents shown on a label on a bottle of mineral water.

ion	contents in mg/dm³	
	sea water	mineral water
chloride	19 300	7.5
sodium	10 700	8.0
sulphate	2 700	6.7
magnesium	1 200	6.0
calcium	400	10.4
others	600	10.2

a What would be the total mass of dissolved solids in 100 cm³ of each type of water? (1 dm³ = 1000 cm³)

b Describe an experiment you could do to check this in the laboratory.

c The ions in river water are in much lower concentrations than in the sea. What process concentrates the ions in sea water?

d The five named ions are all found in similar concentrations in mineral water. Why do the concentrations vary so much in sea water? What removes ions from the sea?

e This mineral water comes from the Auvergne in France. If you have a bottle of mineral water at home, compare the amounts of ions to those in the French water. Why do the concentrations of ions in mineral water vary?

7.4 Carbon dioxide

Key points

- The amount of carbon dioxide in the air has increased dramatically over the last five years.
- This is because of the increase in the burning of fossil fuels.
- There is now concern that the increase in atmospheric carbon dioxide is enhancing the Earth's greenhouse effect and that this may be causing global warming.

1 This table shows some processes which change the amounts of oxygen and carbon dioxide in the air.

a Copy and complete the table. Use these words:

    increases   decreases   stays the same

process	oxygen	carbon dioxide
respiration (animals and plants)		
photosynthesis (plants)		
combustion (fuels)		
corrosion (metals)		

b Use information from the table to explain why the composition of the air has stayed the same for millions of years. How are the activities of humans now causing a change?

2 Suppose global warming causes the Earth to become warmer again.

a Design a page for a holiday brochure showing what it would be like to visit the area where you live.

You need to describe:

- the climate
- the landscape
- local food and plants
- what activities you will be able to do in the area.

b What disadvantages will global warming cause to the way of life for people where you live?

3 This table gives some information about surface temperatures of planets in our solar system.

planet	distance from Sun ($\times 10^6$ km)	surface temperature in °C	
		predicted	actual
Mercury	60	167	167
Venus	110	7	467
Earth	150	-33	17
Moon	150	-33	-33
Mars	230	-68	-63
Jupiter	780	-183	-103

a Would water be a solid, a liquid or a gas on each planet? Explain why this is one reason that astronomers do not believe there is life on any of the other planets.

b Plot a graph of 'predicted' and 'actual' temperatures against distance from the Sun.

Mercury, the Moon and Mars do not have atmospheres. Venus, the Earth and Jupiter all have dense atmospheres.

c What effect does having an atmosphere have on the surface temperature?

d Two students are arguing about the 'greenhouse effect'.

Eve: 'Without the 'greenhouse effect' there would be no life on Earth.'

Pat: 'No, it's caused by pollution. The 'greenhouse effect' could cause mass extinctions.'

Who do you think is right? Write a longer explanation of each person's point of view.

7.5 Rock formation

Key points

- Each type of rock may contain evidence of the conditions under which it was formed.
- Sedimentary rocks may have been deposited in active or quiet conditions.
- Igneous rocks may have formed above or below the surface of the Earth.

- Metamorphic rocks may have formed by the action of both high temperature and high pressure or by the action of high temperature alone.

1 An old quarry has some interesting sedimentary rocks, as shown in the diagram.

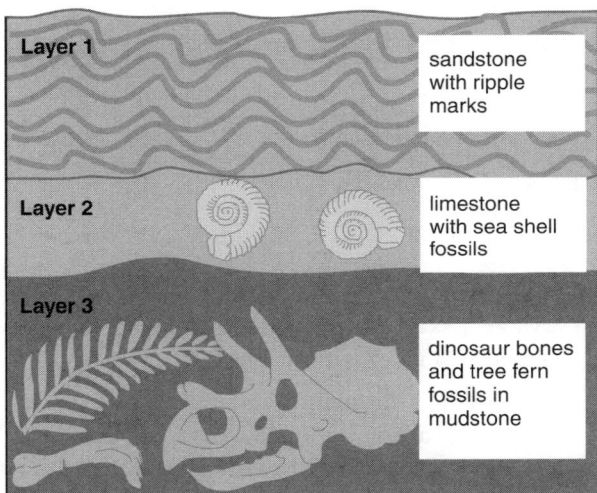

The quarry is going to be opened to the public. Information boards are to be put up to show people what the land used to be like.

a What evidence proves that these rocks are sedimentary rocks?

b Make sketch plans for the information boards. You need to show what the land was like when each rock layer was formed.

A few miles away there is a basalt quarry near a hill which geologists believe is an extinct volcano. Stone from this quarry looks like this when examined under a microscope.

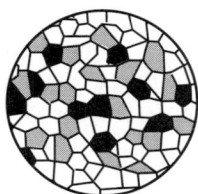

c Design an information board to show how this basalt was formed. Show what the landscape must have looked like at the time.

2 In the middle of the Atlantic Ocean there is a chain of underwater volcanoes. Magma from underneath the Earth's crust pours out and solidifies to make rock.

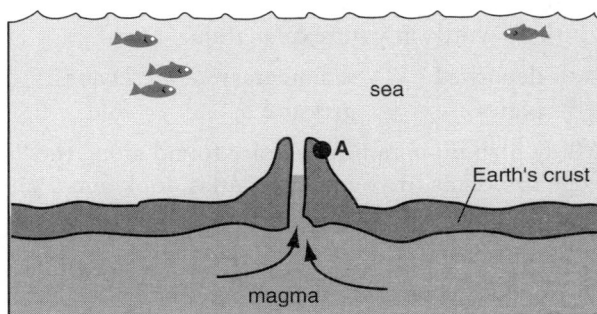

Look at **Point A** on the diagram.

a Which of the following statements are true of rocks at Point A?

  i The rocks contain crystals.
  ii The rocks are formed in layers.
  iii The rocks could be limestone or sandstone.
  iv The rocks are igneous.
  v The rocks are older than surrounding rocks.
  vi The rocks contain the same compounds as molten magma.

These volcanoes are a rich source of ions, including bromide, Br^-, chloride, Cl^- and sulphate, SO_4^{2-}.

b Write the formulae for these compounds which are formed from these ions in the sea. Use the Periodic Table to help you.

  i magnesium sulphate
  ii calcium chloride
  iii potassium sulphate
  iv sodium bromide
  v calcium sulphate
  vi magnesium bromide

7.6 **The rock record**

Key points

- The rock record represents the evidence that is left behind from events in the past that have led to the formation and possible distortion of layers of rocks.
- These layers of rock form a succession.

- Rocks in succession usually become progressively older moving down.
- All of these may provide evidence to help date rocks and suggest what may have happened to them in the past.

1 Mount Everest is the highest mountain in the World. It is 8848 m above the sea – that is nearly 9 kilometres! The top of Mount Everest is made of limestone which contains sea shells.

a Explain, **using diagrams**, how a sea shell came to be in the rock on top of Mount Everest. Use these words in your explanation.

| deposited | sedimentary | layers |
| plates | pressure | fold |

Many high mountain ranges are found along the edge of oceans (if you have an atlas, look and see). For example, the Rockies are along the west coast of North America and are 4400 m high.

b Suppose your class were going on a field trip to North America. Make a list of evidence you would look for to find out if the Rockies were made of pushed up sedimentary rock.

IDEAS AND EVIDENCE

2 This formation of rocks can be seen on the coast of Africa.

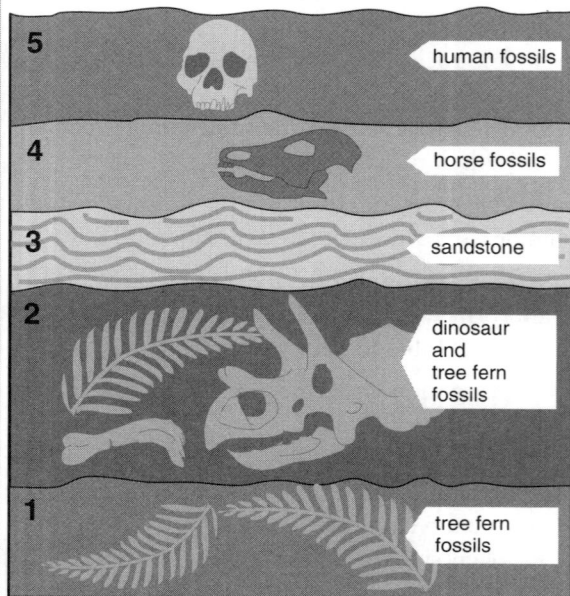

Andy is a palaeontologist (he studies fossils). He dated the fossils in the rocks using 'carbon dating', which can determine the age of the carbon found in things that were once living. Here are the results of the carbon dating of the fossils.

fossil	age in millions of years
tree ferns in deepest layer	300
horse	50
human skull	0.01
mesosaurus dinosaur	200

a Make a sketch copy of the rock layers and label each layer with its age.

b i Why is it difficult to date rock layer 3 using carbon dating?
 ii Estimate the age of rock layer 3. What did you assume so that you could make this estimate?

c Andy already knew that rock layer 1 was the oldest. How did he know this?

d Which of the following ideas does the evidence in the rocks support? Which idea is not supported? Explain your answer.

- Dinosaurs were extinct before horses evolved.
- Tree ferns were extinct before dinosaurs evolved.

e In the nineteenth century, many scientists still believed that fossils were the remains of animals which all died at the same time in a great flood. They thought the only animals to survive had been carried on Noah's Ark. What evidence in the rocks supports this idea? What evidence does not support this idea?

8.1 The Haber process

Key points

- Ammonia is made by the Haber process.
- The Haber process involves a reaction in equilibrium.
- Using the right conditions makes more ammonia.

1 This table shows information about the raw materials needed to make ammonia.

raw material	purpose
air	separated to give nitrogen
methane gas or coal	processed to give hydrogen. Used as energy source for the industrial process
water	cleaning and cooling. Processed with gas or coal to make hydrogen

a Methane is now used much more than coal to make hydrogen. Suggest why.

This is a sketch map of Billingham, where large quantities of ammonia for fertilisers are made.

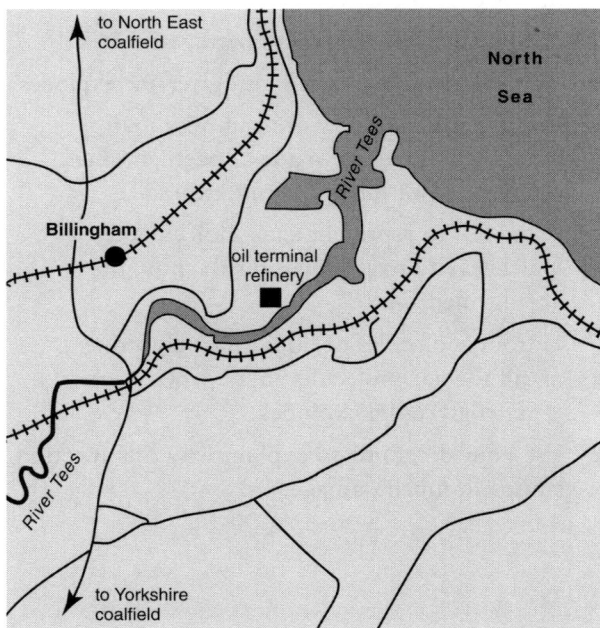

b Explain why Billingham was chosen as a site for industrial production of ammonia. What other factors, apart from availability of raw materials, are important?

2 Nitrogen for the Haber process comes from the air. The air is cooled and then separated through several steps.

Step 1: Air is cooled from 20 °C to – 80 °C. Water forms ice and then carbon dioxide also solidifies.

a Use this information to predict the freezing point of carbon dioxide. Choose from these temperatures:

   0 °C   15 °C   -56 °C   -85 °C

Step 2: The remaining gases are mainly nitrogen and oxygen. They are both liquefied at –200 °C. The gases are separated using fractional distillation.

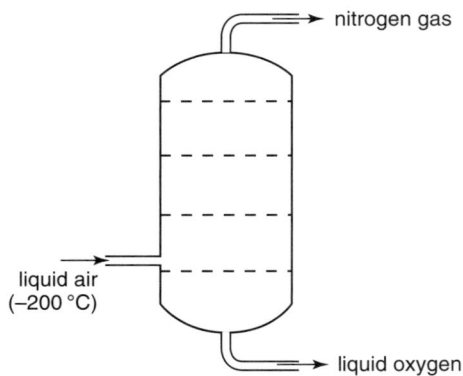

b Which gas, oxygen or nitrogen, has the higher boiling point? Explain your reasoning.

c Predict the boiling points of oxygen and nitrogen. Choose from this list.

   -222 °C   -211 °C   -196 °C   -183 °C

d The oxygen is sold at a much higher price than the nitrogen. Suggest reasons why.

e Why do you think it is important to use pure nitrogen rather than air for the Haber process?

8.2 Nitric acid

Key points

- Ammonia can be oxidised to form nitric acid.
- In industry, nitric acid is made from ammonia.
- Nitric acid is used to make fertilisers and explosives.

1 Use these compounds to answer the following questions:

ammonia   ammonium sulphate
ammonium nitrate   nitric acid

a Whish is a compound of nitrogen and hydrogen only?

b Which reacts with sulphuric acid to form ammonium sulphate?

c Which two are compounds of hydrogen, nitrogen and oxygen?

d Which is a gas at room temperature and pressure that turns damp red litmus blue?

2 Nitric acid is manufactured in a two-step process. In step 1, ammonia and air react together at 900 °C and 10 atm pressure. The gases pass over a hot mesh of platinum and rhodium which is heated by an electric current.

$$4NH_3 + 5O_2 \boxed{} 4NO + 6H_2O$$

a Copy the equation and write a symbol in the box to show that the reaction is reversible. Write the **word** equation underneath.

b Explain why nitric acid can be made much more cheaply if it is made on the same industrial site as ammonia.

c The platinum–rhodium catalyst is very expensive to buy. Explain why buying it makes the process work out cheaper in the long term.

In step 2, the nitrogen monoxide from step 1 is mixed with more air and bubbles up through a tower of water. It reacts to make nitric acid.

$$4NO + 3O_2 + 2H_2O \rightarrow 4HNO_3$$

d Which of these words describe this reaction?

reduction   neutralisation
oxidation   combustion

e Chemical engineers design chemical plants. They need to choose materials which are corrosion resistant and will withstand the conditions of the reactions. What would you need to consider when choosing materials to build a nitric acid plant?

3 Nitric acid is used to make explosives such as nitroglycerine.

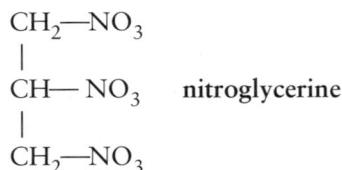

$$\begin{array}{l} CH_2\!-\!NO_3 \\ | \\ CH\!-\!NO_3 \qquad \textbf{nitroglycerine} \\ | \\ CH_2\!-\!NO_3 \end{array}$$

Nitroglycerine explodes even if it is just slightly bumped. It is made safer by mixing it into clay and making the mixture into sticks. This is dynamite, and has to be detonated to make it explode. It can be used to blast rock from quarries. This equation shows what happens when nitroglycerine explodes.

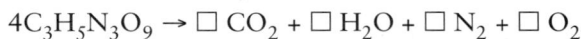

$$4C_3H_5N_3O_9 \rightarrow \square\, CO_2 + \square\, H_2O + \square\, N_2 + \square\, O_2$$

a Copy the equation and balance it by putting numbers in the boxes.

All the products of the reaction are gases.

b Why is water a gas when nitroglycerine explodes?

c Use the equation to work out how many molecules of gas are made altogether when 4 molecules of nitroglycerine explode.

d Using 'O' to represent each molecule, draw 'particles in boxes' diagrams to show the arrangement of:

  i four molecules of liquid nitroglycerine
  ii **all** the gas molecules made when nitroglycerine explodes.

e Use your diagrams to explain why this reaction causes so much damage.

8.3 Fertilisers

Key points

- The need for nitrogen fertiliser has risen.

- One fertiliser can be made by neutralising ammonia with nitric acid.

1 Jo made some ammonium sulphate fertiliser in the school laboratory. These are the instructions she used.

- Measure out $25\,cm^3$ of ammonium hydroxide into a beaker.
- Add a few drops of indicator.
- Add $1\,cm^3$ of acid and stir. Keep adding acid, $1\,cm^3$ at a time, until the indicator changes colour.
- Record the volume of acid added.
- Pour this away. Add exactly the same volume of acid to a fresh $25\,cm^3$ volume of ammonium hydroxide, without indicator.
- This gives you ammonium sulphate solution.

a Which acid would Jo need to use to make ammonium sulphate?

b Explain why Jo had to mix the solutions together twice.

c Draw a diagram to show how Jo could get solid ammonium sulphate from the solution.

d Jo could use a pH meter, instead of indicator, to find out when the ammonium hydroxide is neutralised. What changes in pH would she see during the experiment?

e In a fertiliser factory, a pH meter attached to a computer is a convenient way of following neutralisation.

  i What are the **disadvantages** of using indicator solution for this purpose?

  ii What are the **advantages** of using a pH meter attached to a computer?

2 This table shows some information about some compounds which are used as fertilisers.

name	formula	solubility in water
ammonium sulphate	$(NH_4)_2SO_4$	soluble
ammonium nitrate	NH_4NO_3	very soluble
urea	CON_2H_4	not very soluble

Fertiliser enters plant roots in solution in water.

a Explain why ammonium nitrate is called a 'fast release' fertiliser, and urea is called a 'slow release' fertiliser.

b Explain why ammonium nitrate is usually sold in pellets (large lumps) rather than powder.

c This is how a student worked out the percentage of nitrogen in ammonium nitrate.

Relative formula mass of NH_4NO_3 = 80
Mass of nitrogen = 28
Percentage of nitrogen = $(28 \div 80) \times 100 = 35\%$

Use the same method to work out the percentage of nitrogen in the other two fertilisers.

d Design fertiliser bags for selling urea and ammonium nitrate as fertilisers. Make it clear to customers what **advantages** each fertiliser has. Which would you recommend to farmers for fast-growing wheat? Which would be good for gardeners who want to add fertiliser to their soil only once a year?

8.4 Fertiliser problems

Key points

- Using too much nitrogen-containing fertiliser can cause eutrophication.
- Nitrogenous fertilisers can contaminate drinking water.

1 Farmers spread ammonium nitrate onto their fields as a fertiliser. This table shows what happens to 1 kg of ammonium nitrate after it has been spread onto a field.

washed out of soil	100 g
decomposed	100 g
stays in soil	250 g
used by crop	550 g

a Convert the masses in the table into percentages.

b Draw a pie chart to show what happens to ammonium nitrate after it is spread on the fields.

c Explain why the chart shows that there are **economic** disadvantages of using ammonium nitrate fertiliser.

d Some farmers now use organic rather than chemical fertilisers, because they are worried about the health risks caused by using large amounts of nitrates. Nitrates move slowly through the soil. They move at the rate of about 1 m each year. Groundwater, which enters rivers, is over 20 m underground. In some parts of the UK, the levels of nitrate in drinking water exceed EC limits. High levels of nitrates have been blamed for certain types of cancer and 'blue baby' syndrome.

Write a letter to a farmers' magazine to encourage farmers to 'go organic'. You need to explain:

- how nitrates from chemical fertilisers get into the water supply
- what health risks are caused
- why the problems caused by using large amounts of nitrates will last for decades.

2 Talk to members of your family who enjoy gardening. Find out what their attitude is to using chemicals on their garden. What chemical products do they use? What are the advantages? What are the disadvantages? Make a list of the key points they make.

3 Ions in the soil stick to the surface of clays. Clays are covered with negative charges. Small ions with high positive charges stick most strongly to the negatively charged clay. Ions which do not stick to the clays are most easily washed through the soil. This is a diagram of the surface of clays, showing the relative sizes of some of the ions in the soil.

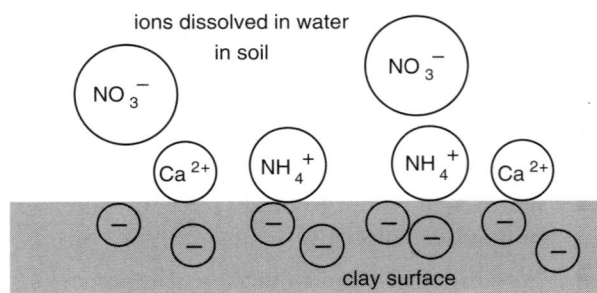

a Explain why nitrate ions do not stick to the clay. Why does this mean that nitrate ions are most easily leached through the soil?

b Give **two** reasons why calcium ions stick more strongly than ammonium ions.

c Ammonium phosphate, $(NH_4)_3PO_4$, is used as a fertiliser.
  i Give the name and formula of the two ions in ammonium phosphate.
  ii Which ion would you expect to leach? Explain your reasoning.

d Do clays in soil lessen the problems of eutrophication? Explain your answer.

A1.1 Water as a solvent

Key points

- Sea water contains dissolved sodium chloride and other salts.
- The solubility of salts in water can be measured.
- For most substances, solubility increases with increase in temperature.

---

1 A book gives advice about how to survive in the desert. It says you can get water by:

- spreading a plastic sheet across the sand
- weighing down the sheet with stones
- collecting any water that condenses in the beaker.

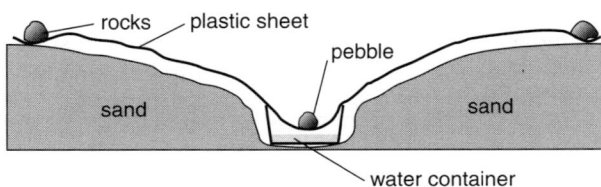

a Make a copy of the diagram and label it with these labels.

   $H_2O(l)$ $H_2O(g)$
   evaporation   condensation

b The book suggests that you can soak the sand with your own urine to make sure no water is wasted. The water will still be safe to drink. Do you think this is true? Explain your reasoning.

c Some students tried out this method on a cold day on the local beach. They did not manage to collect very much water. Make a list of suggestions to show how the set up could be changed to collect the most water possible.

---

2 Design an experiment to prove that fizzy lemonade contains:

- dissolved gases, including carbon dioxide
- dissolved sugar
- water.

Write a clear set of instructions for another pupil to follow. Say what results you expect.

---

3 Asha heated up some copper sulphate crystals in a test tube until all the water of crystallisation had evaporated.

   $CuSO_4.5H_2O(s) \rightarrow CuSO_4(s) + 5H_2O(g)$

The copper sulphate changed colour from blue to white.

a What else would Asha **see** during the reaction?

b How could she prove that the colour change happened because the copper sulphate had lost water?

c Asha weighed the test tube before and after heating. What do you expect had happened to the mass? Explain your answer.

---

4 This table gives some data about the solubilities of sodium chloride and potassium nitrate at different temperatures.

temperature in °C	solubility in g/100 g	
	NaCl	KNO$_3$
0	35	15
10	35	20
20	35	32
30	35	50
40	35	74

a Plot a graph to show to show the solubility curve for each salt.

b Describe how the solubility of potassium nitrate changes with temperature.

c Why is the solubility of sodium chloride unusual?

d Describe how you get a pure sample of potassium nitrate from a solid mixture of equal amounts of potassium nitrate and sodium chloride.

A1.2 **Water hardness**

Key points

- Hardness in water is caused by dissolved calcium and magnesium salts.

- Water hardness can be temporary or permanent.
- Hardness can be removed from water.

---

1 In remote areas, water supplies for houses are sometimes taken directly from local streams. This is a map of an area where drinking water is taken from the streams at sites A to E.

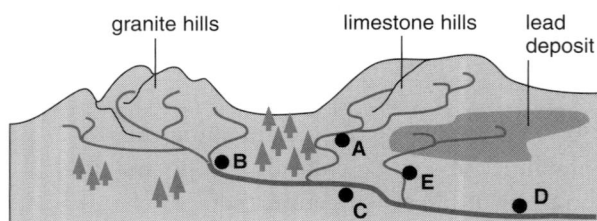

a Which sites have hard water?

b The water at point E contains dissolved lead. Why is this water not safe to drink?

c One of the local people suggested that if the water from site E was boiled it would be safe to drink. Do you agree? Explain your reasoning.

---

2 Stalactites are long columns of limestone rock which are formed in underground caves. This is an explanation, taken from a chemistry text book, which explains how they form.

Acidic rain water at 20° C dissolves surface limestone. The saturated solution trickles through the underground cave. The temperature of the cave is 10° C, which causes some calcium carbonate to precipitate out, forming stalactites.

a Explain the meaning of the terms **saturated solution** and **precipitates out**.

b Why is the temperature change so important to this process?

---

3 Sue carried out some experiments to find out the best way of softening tap water from her house. She used five samples of tap water, all from the same tap, which she treated in different ways. She measured how much soap was needed to make a good lather (hard water needs more soap to make a lather).

sample	treatment	volume of soap needed in cm^3
A	none	8
B	boiling	6.5
C	distilling	0.5
D	ion exchange	0.5
E	adding sodium carbonate	0.5

a Why did Sue test sample A without treating it first?

b What type of hardness is in the water from Sue's house:

- temporary
- permanent
- both temporary and permanent?

Explain your reasoning.

c What substances are dissolved in Sue's tap water? Explain, using equations, how they came to be there.

d Sodium carbonate used to be called 'washing soda'. The Victorians softened water for washing clothes by adding 'washing soda'. Why do you think this method of softening water was more commonly used than any other?

A1.3 Water hardness problems

Key points

- Soap can be used to measure the amount of hardness in water.

- Hard water can have both disadvantages and advantages.

---

1 Hard water causes a build up of scale on the inside of pipes.

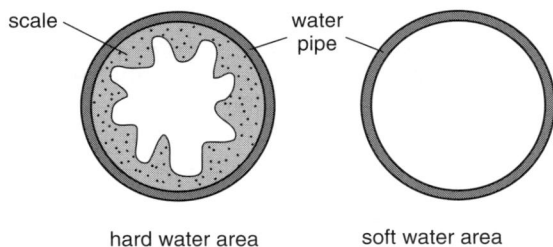

scale — water pipe

hard water area   soft water area

a In some areas, water pipes are made from lead, which is toxic. Having hard water in these areas is an advantage. Explain why.

b New water pipes are often made from plastic. Draw an advert for a company which sells plastic water pipes. Include in your advert a list of advantages of replacing lead pipes with plastic pipes.

c Farms and large greenhouses have systems of pipes for watering plants. One way of removing limescale from the pipes is to flush them with nitric acid.

   i What is the chemical name for limescale?
   ii Write a symbol equation for the reaction between the limescale and the acid.
   iii Why do you think nitric acid is a better acid to use for pipes which carry water for crops, rather than hydrochloric or sulphuric acid?
   iv Nitric acid should not be used for pipes at home. Give some reasons why.

2 One symptom of limescale in pipes at home is that the water runs slowly from the hot taps. Make a survey of your own home. Is your water hard or soft? What evidence can you see to prove this?

3 Hard water makes a scum when it is shaken with soap solution. One way of measuring how much scum is formed is by using a colorimeter. A colorimeter measures how much light is transmitted through a test-tube. The more scum, the less light can get through.

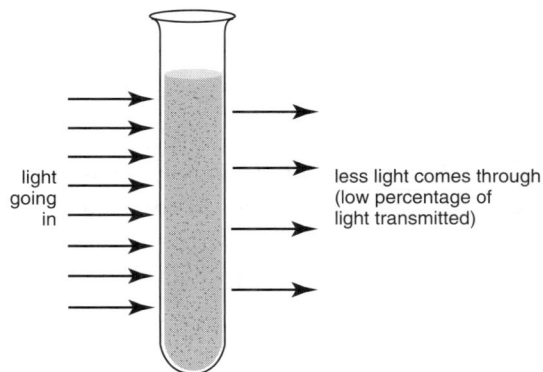

light going in → less light comes through (low percentage of light transmitted)

This is a set of results an experiment. Soap solution was mixed with a sample of hard water, and the amount of light transmitted through the test-tube was measured.

volume of soap solution added in cm³	percentage of light transmitted
0.0	100
1.0	93
2.0	84
3.0	75
4.0	68
5.0	61
6.0	52

a Plot the results on a graph.

b Explain what happens to the percentage of light transmitted as more soap is added to the sample. Why does this happen?

c Detergents, such as shampoos, do not make scum. Sketch a line on your graph to show what the results would look like if the experiment was repeated using detergent.

d What further experiments would you need to do to find out if the water had temporary or permanent hardness?

A2.1 **Acids and alkalis**

Key points

- The characteristic feature of an acid is that it contains a hydrogen atom that is replaceable.
- When acids dissolve in water they produce hydrogen ions, H^+.
- The strength of an acid depends on the amount to which it ionises.

- The concentration of an acid depends on the amount of it that is dissolved in water.
- The strength of an alkali depends on the extent to whcih it produces OH^- ions when it is dissolved in water.

---

1 Look at the list of facts about acids and alkalis shown below. Copy and complete the table to show which facts are only true of acids, which are only true of alkalis and which are true for both.

fact	true for acid	true for alkali	true for both

- Form OH^- ions in water.
- Are corrosive.
- Are ionic compounds.
- Taste bitter.
- Have a pH greater than 7.
- React with carbonates.
- Form salts.
- Can be weak or strong.
- Form H^+ ions in water.
- Change the colour of neutral Universal Indicator paper.
- Conduct electricity when dissolved in water.

2

a Draw diagrams to show the structure of:
  i a hydrogen atom
  ii a hydrogen ion.
b Use your diagrams to explain why acids are sometimes called '*proton donors*'.

---

3 This diagram shows the pH of a range of household and laboratory substances.

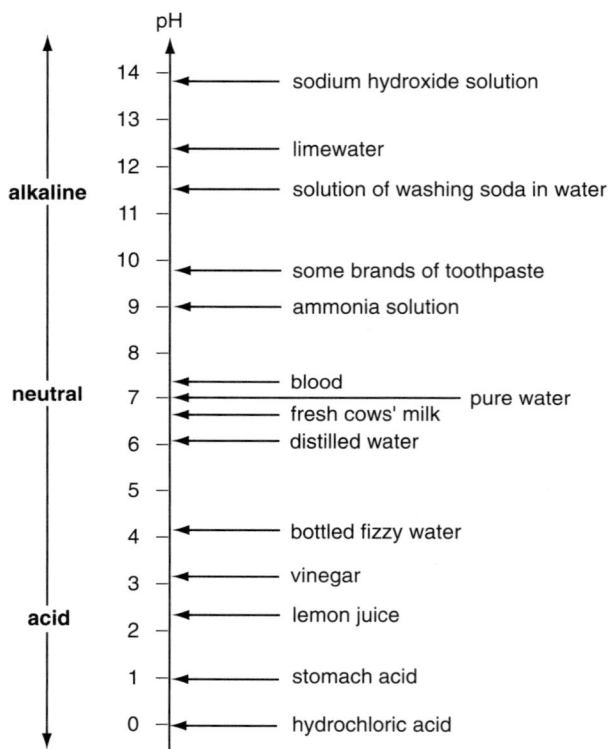

(Artwork © Andrew Hunt and Alan Sykes, reprinted by permission of Pearson Education Limited.)

a Which substance is the strongest alkali?

b Which substance is the weakest acid?

c Name three substances which form H^+ ions when they dissolve in water.

d Which acid ionises the most easily?

e Suppose you had spilled some household ammonia at home. Suggest another household substance you could use to neutralise it.

f Some people treat ant bites with baking powder (sodium hydrogencarbonate). What does this tell you about ant bites?

A2.2 Salts

Key points

- Acids and alkalis react together in neutralisation reactions.
- The progress of a neutralisation reaction can be following the change in heat, in the conductivity or in the colour of an indicator as the reaction takes place.
- Neutralisation reactions can be used to make salts.

---

1   Ann carried out a titration. She put 25 cm³ of hydrochloric acid into a beaker, and ran sodium hydroxide solution into the beaker from a burette. This graph shows how the temperature changed.

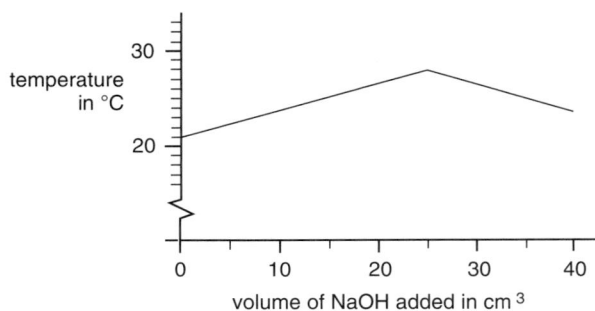

a   Draw a fully labelled diagram to show the equipment Ann needed to do this experiment.

She wrapped the beaker in polystyrene for insulation.

b   Why did she need to insulate the beaker?

c   What volume of sodium hydroxide neutralised the acid? What does this tell you about the concentration of the sodium hydroxide and the hydrochloric acid?

d   Explain why Ann did not need to use an indicator in this titration.

e   Make a sketch copy of the graph. Sketch other lines on the graph to show what the shape of the graph would be if:

  i She used 20 cm³ hydrochloric acid.

  ii She added water to the sodium hydroxide solution before she put it into the burette.

2   This is a newspaper report of an accident at a chemical factory.

FIREMAN CALLED TO ACID SPILL

Firemen were called to TS Chemicals yesterday after a large spill of hydrochloric acid from a drum at the factory. Steel machinery was badly damaged. The chief fire officer said that the open windows and doors had saved the factory from the risk of explosion. Firemen wearing breathing apparatus used soda ash to neutralise the acid and hosed down the whole area with water.

---

a   Steel contains mostly iron. Write a word equation for the reaction of hydrochloric acid with iron. Why does this reaction mean that there was a risk of explosion after the acid spill?

b   Soda ash contains sodium carbonate. Write a symbol equation to show how the soda ash reacts with hydrochloric acid.

c   What gas would be made when the soda ash neutralised the acid? Why might this be a danger to the firemen?

d   Describe two ways the firemen could find out whether the acid was fully neutralised.

e   Make a list of all the hazards the firemen faced at each stage in the clean up operation. Make suggestions about what safety precautions they should have taken at each stage.

A2.3 Precipitation

Key points

- Some salts are insoluble in water.
- Insoluble salts are made by precipitation.
- Precipitation reactions can be used to identify some ions.

1 Silver bromide is used to make photographic films. Lee made some silver bromide by a precipitation reaction. He mixed a solution of silver nitrate with a solution of potassium bromide.

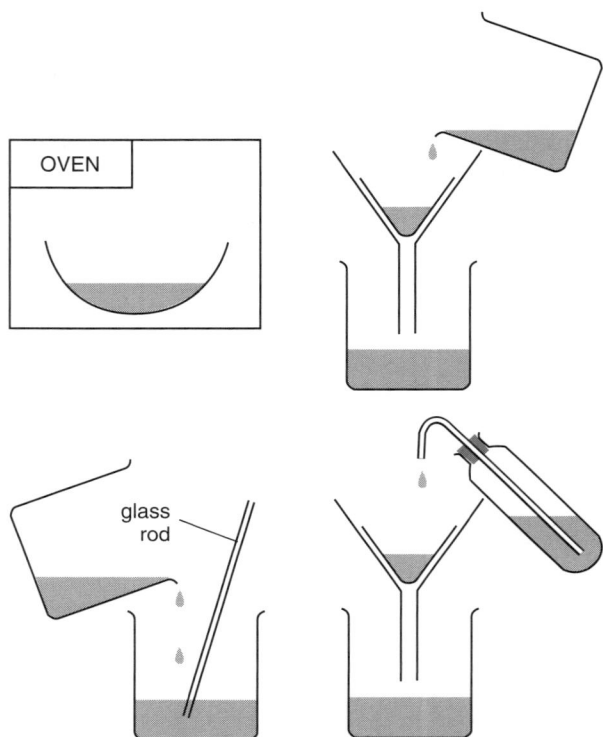

a Put the diagrams into the right order and copy them into your book. Label the steps 'Step 1' to 'Step 4'. Leave plenty of space for labels.

b Write these labels on your diagrams:
- distilled water
- silver nitrate solution
- impure residue of silver bromide
- clean, dry silver bromide
- potassium bromide solution

c Lee tested the water after it had been used to wash the silver bromide in Step 3. He found that it made a creamy precipitate when he added a few drops of silver nitrate solution. Why do you think this happened?

2 Alex made some barium sulphate by mixing together solutions of barium nitrate, $Ba(NO_3)_2$ and sodium sulphate, Na_2SO_4. The diagrams below show what the particles look like in the beakers of barium nitrate (before mixing) and barium sulphate (after mixing).

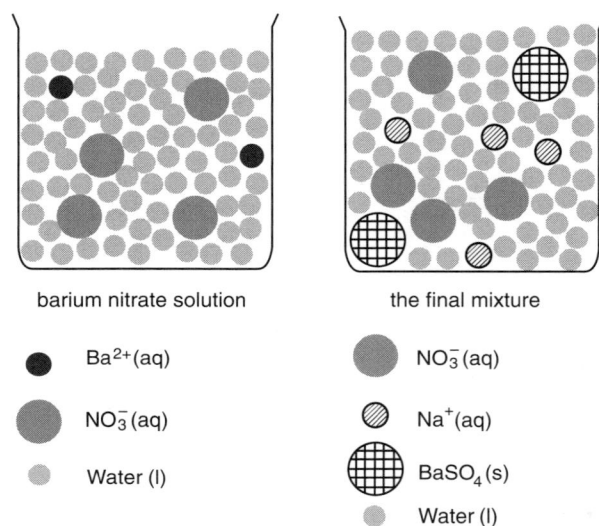

barium nitrate solution   the final mixture

- $Ba^{2+}(aq)$
- $NO_3^-(aq)$
- Water (l)

- $NO_3^-(aq)$
- $Na^+(aq)$
- $BaSO_4(s)$
- Water (l)

a Draw a similar diagram to show what the particles look like in sodium sulphate solution (before mixing).

b What are the *spectator ions* in this reaction?

c A 'barium meal' is sometimes given to people in hospitals before they have an X-ray. This fills up the stomach so that it can be clearly seen. Barium ions are very toxic. Explain why people can safely swallow barium sulphate, even though barium ions are toxic.

3 Silver bromide is used to make photographic films. In a chemical factory, potassium bromide and silver nitrate react to make a precipitate of silver bromide.

a What is the waste product of the reaction?

b One way of disposing of waste from these factories is to put it directly into local rivers. What environmental and economic problems would this cause?

A3.1 Alloys

Key points

- A mixture of metals is called an alloy.
- Alloys have different properties from pure metals.
- Alloys have many uses related to their properties.

1 A book states that 'An alloy is formed when two or more metals are mixed together.' John uses a coarse file firstly on a lump of scrap iron and then on some chromium. He collects together all the tiny bits and mixes them together. What else must be done before this mixture can correctly be called an alloy?

2 Brass is an alloy used to make the metal prongs of three-pin electrical plugs, which fit into the wall sockets. The main constituent of brass is copper.

a Name the other element found in brass.

b What is the property of copper and brass which lets them both be used in electric plugs?

c What is the advantage of making the prongs from brass instead of copper?

d Suggest why the wires which carry the electricity to the plug are made from copper instead of brass.

3 Make a table to show the elements present in each of the following alloys. Give the main uses of each alloy. **bronze   stainless steel   solder**

4 The alloy duralumin contains aluminium and copper. It is denser than pure aluminium but stronger than either aluminium or copper separately. The table shows the relative strength of the alloys made by chill casting (rapid cooling of the molten alloy) or sand casting (slow cooling of the molten alloy) for alloys containing different percentages of aluminium and copper, compared with pure aluminium.

a Use graph paper to plot the relative strength of the alloy (y-axis) against the percentage of copper in each type of alloy (x-axis). Draw both graphs on the same axes. Label one 'chill cast' and the other 'sand cast'. Plot the graph lines as smooth curves. You should find that each contains a peak.

percentage of copper in alloy	relative strength of alloy (chill cast)	relative strength of alloy (sand cast)
0	1.0	1.0
2	1.2	1.2
4	1.4	1.4
6	1.6	1.6
8	2.0	1.8
10	3.0	2.5
12	2.4	1.9
14	1.8	1.4
16	1.4	1.1

b Which method (chill casting or sand casting) produces the strongest alloy?

c What percentage of copper is in the strongest alloy?

d How many times stronger is the alloy in c than pure aluminium?

e What percentages of copper produce sand cast alloys twice as strong as pure aluminium?

f Use ideas about the arrangement of particles and the relative sizes of copper and aluminium atoms to explain why the alloys are stronger than either pure aluminium or pure copper.

g Suggest why a sand cast alloy is never stronger than a chill cast alloy containing the same percentages of elements. (Hint! Use ideas of rate of cooling to answer this.)

h A duralumin manufacturer wants to produce a chill cast alloy which has a relative strength of 2 compared with pure aluminium.

i What percentages of copper in duralumin will give this strength?

ii Assume that the cost of producing copper is £1000 per tonne and aluminium is £750 per tonne. Work out the cost of producing 1 tonne of each of the two types of aluminium in part i. Which one is the more economical to produce?

A3.2 Rusting

- Iron must be in contact with both oxygen and water to rust.
- Rusting can be prevented in a number of ways.

1 Suggest a reason for each of the following.

a An iron nail would not rust on the Moon's surface.

b A crashed car would rust only very slowly in the Sahara Desert.

c A crashed car would rust quite quickly in an English river.

2

a What is meant by the term 'galvanised iron'?

b How is an iron object such as a bucket made into galvanised iron?

c What is the advantage of using a bucket that has been galvanised rather than one which is made just from iron?

d Zinc is higher than iron in the reactivity series. Suggest why it protects the iron from rusting, even when the bucket is scratched.

3 Here is part of the reactivity series for the metals zinc, iron, tin and lead, relative to hydrogen. The higher the metal, the easier it is for that metal to displace hydrogen from an acid.

most reactive   zinc
           iron
           tin
least reactive   lead
           (hydrogen)

The cans in which foods are stored have to resist the attack of the very weak acids in the food. These cans are made from mild steel that has been given a protective coating.

a Suggest why a food can uses a tin coating inside it instead of a lead coating.

b Explain why a mild steel can which is coated with zinc does not start to rust when opened.

c Explain why a mild steel can which is coated with tin will start to rust quite quickly.

4 Here is a list of methods by which a steel article could be protected against rust formation.

- Paint it.
- Galvanise it.
- Cover it with oil or grease.
- Coat it with a sacrificial metal.
- Coat it with a less reactive metal which has a decorative finish.

Choose the best method for protecting the following steel articles against rust formation, giving a reason for each of your choices:

a underground oil pipes

b a shed roof

c crash barriers down the middle of motorway

d a tea pot

e a fence.

5 Houses fitted with older style central heating may have radiators and pipes made from mild steel or iron. If the pipes are replaced by modern copper ones connected to these radiators, the radiators may start to rust and leak. Explain why this happens.

IDEAS AND EVIDENCE

6

a Some racing cars use engines made from aluminium instead of steel. The car shells and bodywork are made from fibreglass strengthened with a resin mesh. Suggest why aluminium and fibre glass are used instead of steel.

b The use of aluminium engines in family cars is increasing though the main car structures are still often made from galvanised and painted mild steel. A rubber mount is put between the engine and the steel. The rubber helps to absorb any vibrations, but what other important function does it play?

c It is slightly more expensive to make stainless steel (containing iron, chromium and nickel) than mild steel (containing iron and carbon). The price for a car made from stainless steel is far more than one made from mild steel. Assuming that the manufacturing costs are constant, suggest why.

A3.3 **Redox**

> ### Key points
>
> H ▪ A redox reaction involves both reduction and oxidation.
> H ▪ Redox reactions can involve transfer of electrons.
>
> H ▪ Oxidation is gain of electrons and reduction is loss of electrons.
> H ▪ Displacement reactions are redox reactions.

1 When lead(II) oxide is heated on a charcoal block with a hot flame, tiny silvery balls of metal are set free. A gas, which turns limewater cloudy, is released. The symbol (unbalanced) equation for the reaction is:

$$PbO + C \rightarrow Pb + CO_2$$

a In this reaction, state clearly what has been oxidised and what it has been oxidised to.

b In this reaction, state clearly what has been reduced and what it has been reduced to.

c Copy out and balance the equation.

d What is the name of the gas which turns limewater cloudy?

e What substance is produced which causes the cloudiness?

2 The following reactions involve oxidation and reduction. State clearly what oxidation and reduction is taking place.

a sodium hydroxide + iron(II) chloride →
iron(II) hydroxide + sodium chloride

b carbon + carbon monoxide → carbon dioxide

c lithium hydroxide + lead(II) nitrate →
lead(II) hydroxide + lithium nitrate

3 Explain what happens in oxidation and reduction reactions in terms of electron transfer.

4 For each of the following reactions state clearly the oxidation and reduction which is taking place.

a $Ag_2O + H_2 \rightarrow 2Ag + H_2O$

b $Cl_2 + 2KI \rightarrow 2KCl + I_2$

c $Zn + CuSO_4 \rightarrow Cu + ZnSO_4$

d $Mg + H_2SO_4 \rightarrow MgSO_4 + H_2$

5 Write ionic equations for the following reactions. For each one, explain carefully the oxidation and reduction taking place.

a $Mg + 2HCl \rightarrow MgCl_2 + H_2$

b $2FeCl_2 + Cl_2 \rightarrow 2FeCl_3$

c $Zn + 2AgNO_3 \rightarrow Zn(NO_3)_2 + 2Ag$

d $Br_2 + 2KI \rightarrow 2KBr + I_2$

e $Mg + FeO \rightarrow MgO + Fe$

f $CuO + H_2 \rightarrow Cu + H_2O$

6 Here are the equations for some redox reactions.

a Name the reducing agent in each reaction and state what happens to it.

  i $Cl_2 + 2LiI \rightarrow 2LiCl + I_2$
  ii $3Ca + Fe_2O_3 \rightarrow 3 CaO + 2Fe$
  iii $Mg + ZnO \rightarrow MgO + Zn$

b Name the oxidising agent in each reaction and state what happens to it.

  i $Fe + 2HCl \rightarrow FeCl_2 + H_2$
  ii $C + ZnO \rightarrow Zn + CO$
  iii $Mg + CuSO_4 \rightarrow MgSO_4 + Cu$

7 When a copper brooch is to be plated with silver, electrolysis is used. A piece of pure silver is used as the positive electrode, and the brooch is used as the negative electrode. The electrolyte is a solution of a suitable silver salt.

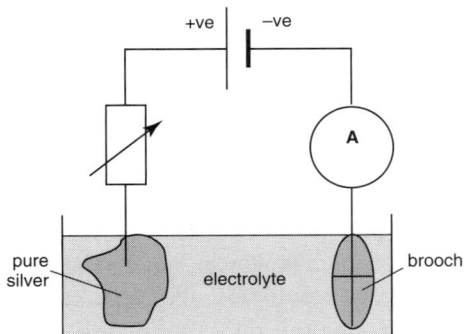

a Write an ion-electron equation to show what happens at the positive electrode and explain why this is an example of oxidation.

b Write an ionic equation to show what happens at the negative electrode and explain why this is an example of reduction.

A4.1 Carbon compounds

1 Propanone is a solvent. It is used in nail polish remover. This is the displayed formula of propanone.

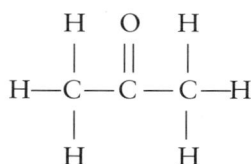

$$
\begin{array}{ccc}
\text{H} & \text{O} & \text{H} \\
| & || & | \\
\text{H—C} & \text{—C} & \text{—C—H} \\
| & & | \\
\text{H} & & \text{H}
\end{array}
$$

a A bottle of nail polish remover has the following warning.

WARNING
Very flammable.
Keep away from polished surfaces

i Why does propanone damage polished surfaces?

ii What gases will be formed when propanone burns?

A cosmetic company were developing cotton wool pads soaked with nail polish remover as a new product. The company wanted a more oily nail polish remover because the propanone evaporated off the pads too quickly. The company's research chemist suggested that they try butanone.

b Draw the displayed formula of butanone.

c Butanone is more oily than propanone and evaporates less easily. Explain why.

d Two test tubes contain a sample of butanone and propanone. Describe **two** ways you could find out which is which. What safety precautions would you need to take when you were carrying out the experiments?

2 The carboxylic acids are a homologous series. They have the general formula $C_nH_{2n+1}COOH$. The formula for ethanoic acid is CH_3COOH.

a What is the formula for propanoic acid?

b What is the formula for octanoic acid (contains a total of 8 carbon atoms)?

c What is the name of this acid?

C_3H_7COOH

Ethanoic acid is the acid found in vinegar.

Ethanoic acid is a weak acid. This is the equation for the dissociation of ethanoic acid:

$$CH_3COOH \rightarrow CH_3COO^- + H^+$$

d How does the equation show that ethanoic acid behaves like a typical acid?

e When ethanoic acid reacts with sodium hydroxide, it makes a salt called sodium ethanoate. What is the formula of sodium ethanoate? (Look at the equation to help you).

3 Esters are formed when an alcohol reacts with an acid. The other product is water.

Ethyl ethanoate, $CH_3COOC_2H_5$, is an ester.

a Write down the name of the acid used to make ethyl ethanoate.

b Write down the name of the alcohol used to make ethyl ethanoate.

c Write a balanced equation for the reaction to form ethyl ethanoate.

A4.2 Isomerism

Key points

- Carbon chains can have branches.
- This means that it is possible for two different structures to have the same molecular formula.
- When two different structures have the same molecular formula they are called structural isomers of each other.

1 Petrol in a car engine can 'auto-ignite'. This means it explodes suddenly before the spark plug has sparked, causing 'knocking' in the engine. Until recently, lead compounds were added to petrol to stop 'knocking'.

a Why do we no longer use leaded petrol?

Knocking is caused by straight chain alkanes such as heptane, C_7H_{16}.

$CH_3-CH_2-CH_2-CH_2-CH_2-CH_2-CH_3$

b Why is heptane called a 'straight chain alkane'?

Iso-octane is the old fashioned name for a 'branched chain' isomer of octane which did not cause knocking. The more iso-octane in the petrol, the less knocking. Old fashioned four star petrol had a 'high octane rating'. Modern, unleaded petrol also contains a high percentage of iso-octane.

iso-octane

c Why is iso-octane a 'branched chain' alkane?

d Draw two other possible structures for branched chain molecules which are isomers of octane.

e This is a ring molecule based on octane, which also reduces engine knocking.

What is the formula of cyclo-octane? Explain why this is not a 'true' isomer of octane.

Branched chain alkanes are produced by 'reforming' straight chain alkanes. This is carried out in an oil refinery, at high temperatures, using a platinum catalyst.

f Give one similarity and one difference between reforming and cracking.

2 Which two of these compounds are isomers?

3 The following table shows information about some bromoalkanes.

name	formula
bromomethane	CH_3Br
bromoethane	C_2H_5Br
dibromoethane	$C_2H_4Br_2$
bromopropane	C_3H_7Br
	C_4H_9Br

a All of the compounds in the table belong to the same homologous series except one.

Which one?

b Name the compound with the formula C_4H_9Br.

c Draw the displayed structural formula of two isomers of bromopropane.

d Draw the displayed structural formula of two isomers of dibromoethane.

A4.3 Ethanol

- Ethanol has many uses, including as a solvent, as a fuel and as an alcoholic beverage.
- It is produced on a large scale by fermentation and from ethene.
- The use that the ethanol is to be put to largely determines its method of manufacture.
- Ethanol can be dehydrated to ethene.

1 Some countries, such as Brazil, use ethanol as a fuel for cars. It is blended with petrol or diesel. The ethanol is made by fermenting raw sugar cane. The sugar cane is crushed, and the watery juices are mixed with yeast. The mixture stands in large fermenting vessels, where the warm climate keeps it at about 30 °C. The sugar is made into ethanol.

$$C_6H_{12}O_6 \rightarrow 2C_2H_5OH + 2CO_2$$

a If the vessels get too hot, the reaction stops. Explain why.

b The reaction stops when there is about 7% ethanol in the solution.

  i Why is the ethanol not suitable to use as a fuel in this form?

  ii Suggest what is done to the ethanol before it can be used for fuel.

c Companies in Brazil make large profits from making ethanol for fuel. This would not be possible in the UK. Give at least **two** reasons why making ethanol for fuel would not make a profit in this country.

The same reaction is used in this country to make beer and to make bread rise. Look again at the equation for fermentation.

d Why does yeast make bread rise?

e At the Bass brewery in Burton on Trent, there are large stuffed owls on top of the big fermentation tanks. These frighten small birds away. If the small birds fly over the tanks they suffocate and fall out of the sky to their deaths. Explain why this happens.

2 Methanol is another alcohol. It contains one carbon atom in each molecule.

a Draw the displayed formula of methanol.

b Methanol can be produced from carbon monoxide and hydrogen. Write a symbol equation for the reaction.

3 A chemical company which makes ethanol has a briefing sheet for new employees which contains the following information.

> In the UK, ethanol for industrial use is manufactured by the reaction of ethene with steam at 600 °C and 60 atm pressure.

a Why is ethanol needed 'for industrial use'?

b Explain why the conditions of temperature and pressure are chosen.

The information also explains why a catalyst is used.

> A phosphoric acid catalyst is used in the process. This increases profitability and conserves energy resources.

c Explain why using a catalyst 'increases profitability' and 'conserves energy resources'.

d This is the displayed formula for ethanol.

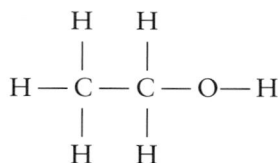

Use displayed formula to write the equation for the industrial manufacture of ethanol.

e This reaction is exothermic. Use ideas about breaking and making bonds to explain why.

A5.1 Formulae and the mole

Key points

- The simplest formula of a compound can be calculated from the percentage composition of that compound.
- The simplest formula shows the simplest ratio of atoms in the compound.
- The molecular formula of a compound shows the actual number of each type of atom present in the compound.

- The formula mass of a substance, in grams, is called one mole of that substance.
- One mole of any substance contains the same number of particles; this is called the Avogadro number.

1 Two ores of copper are cuprite and tenorite. Cuprite contains copper(II) oxide, CuO. Tenorite contains copper(I) oxide, Cu_2O. Both oxides can be reduced to copper by heating them in a stream of hydrogen.

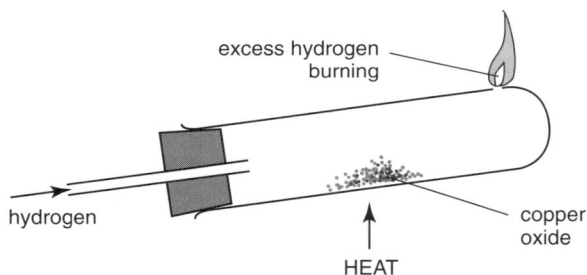

a⟩ Write symbol equations to show what happens when each form of copper oxide is reduced by hydrogen to form copper and water.

b Why is water not seen in the tube during the reaction?

c Why is this called a 'redox' reaction?

d This is a set of results from this experiment.

Mass of copper oxide = 7.2 g
Mass of copper at end = 6.4 g

i Calculate the mass of oxygen lost.
ii Use this to work out the simplest formula of the copper oxide.
iii Which ore does it come from?

e⟩ Carbon powder can also be used to reduce copper oxide. Explain why using it in this experiment would lead to inaccurate results.

2 A chemist is trying to find out what plastic has been used to make a shampoo bottle. These are the results of one experiment.

Carbon content: 85.7 %
Hydrogen content: 14.3 %

a Use these results to work out the simplest formula of the plastic.

b⟩ Which **two** of these plastics could the shampoo bottle be made from?

Polyethene $-(-CH_2-CH_2-)_n-$

Polypropene $-(-CH(CH_3)-CH_2-)_n-$

Polystyrene $-(-CH(C_6H_5)-CH_2-)_n-$

c⟩ Explain why you cannot tell which of the two plastics have been used to make the shampoo bottle.

3⟩ A hydrocarbon contains 82.8% carbon, and has a molecular mass of 58. Work out:

a its simple formula

b molecular formula

c the name of the hydrocarbon.

A5.2 Using the mole

H The number of moles of a substance can be calculated from a given mass of a particular substance and the mass of 1 mole of that substance.

H One mole of any gas always has a volume of 24 dm^3 at room temperature and pressure.

H Balanced chemical equations can be used to calculate quantities of reacting substances and products formed by using the mole concept.

H The concentration of liquids is expressed in terms of moles per decimeter^3 (mol/dm^3).

1

a How many moles of water molecules are in an ice cube which has a mass of 9 g?

b How many single water molecules are in the ice cube? (1 mole is 6 x 10^{23})

c How many hydrogen atoms are in the ice cube?

2 For each of the following pairs of substances, work out which has the highest mass. Use the Periodic Table to help you. Show your working.

a 1 mole of sulphur atoms or 1 mole of oxygen atoms

b 1 mole of carbon atoms or 2 moles of neon atoms

c 1 mole of water molecules or 2 moles of oxygen molecules, O_2

d 2 moles of oxygen molecules, O_2 or 1 mole of sulphur atoms

e 1.5 moles of nitrogen molecules, N_2, or 1 mole of carbon dioxide molecules, CO_2

3 Calcium carbonate, $CaCO_3$, forms calcium oxide, CaO, when it is heated.

a What gas is made at the same time?

b Write a symbol equation for the reaction.

c Work out the mass of one mole of calcium carbonate and calcium oxide. Use the Periodic Table to help you.

d A student heated 20 g of calcium carbonate in the laboratory. How much calcium oxide would be made?

The same reaction is used on a large scale to make calcium oxide for cement making. Limestone is used as a raw material. Limestone is almost pure calcium carbonate. A cement works orders 224 tonnes of calcium oxide. Use these steps to work out how much limestone would need to be heated to make this amount.

e How much limestone would need to be heated to make 56 tonnes of calcium oxide? (1 tonne = 1000 kg)

f How much limestone would need to be heated to make 224 tonnes of calcium oxide?

g In industry, the amount of calcium oxide actually formed is always less than the theoretical amount. Give some reasons why.

4 For each pair of substances, work out which has more moles of atoms. Use the Periodic Table to help you. Show your working.

a 19 g of fluorine atoms or 22 g of boron atoms

b 64 g of sulphur atoms or 64 g of copper atoms

c 2 moles of oxygen atoms or 60 g of argon atoms

d 48 dm^3 of oxygen molecules or 48 g oxygen molecules. (1 mole of gas has a volume of 24 dm^3 under standard conditions.)

5 What is the volume of 16 g of each of the following gases? (1 mole of gas has a volume of 24 dm^3 under standard conditions.)

a oxygen molecules

b sulphur dioxide

c methane.

A5.3 Volumetric analysis

Key points

- In order to measure volumes of liquids accurately, chemists use specialised equipment.
- The use of this equipment enables a comparison of reacting quantities of liquids and solutions to be made.

- The results can be processed to enable calculations of unknown concentrations to be made by the use of substance of known concentration.

---

1 Bobby carried out a titration in school. He wrote up the instructions for homework.

1. Fill a burette with hydrochloric acid (1.0 mol/dm^3), making sure you can reach the top by standing on tip toe.
2. Use a 500 cm^3 measuring cylinder to measure 25 cm^3 of dilute sodium hydroxide into a conical flask.
3. Put 10 cm^3 of indicator into the burette.
4. Turn on the tap of the burette so that the acid runs into the flask.
5. Turn it off when the indicator has changed colour.
6. Write down the result and pack away.

a Copy this table and complete it to show Bobby's mistakes.

mistake	correct instruction
standing on tip toe	use a funnel and keep top of burette below eye level

b Give **three reasons** why following Bobby's instructions would give inaccurate results.

2

a Work out the number of moles of acid in each of these solutions.

   i   100 cm^3 of hydrochloric acid (1.0 mol/dm^3)

   ii 25 cm^3 of sulphuric acid (2.0 mol/dm^3)

   iii 50 cm^3 of nitric acid (0.5 mol/dm^3)

   iv 200 cm^3 of sulphuric acid (4.0 mol/dm^3).

b What **mass** of sulphuric acid is in the solution in part **iv**? (The mass of 1 mole of sulphuric acid is 98).

---

3 Kim carried out a titration to find out the concentration of some sodium hydroxide solution. She used 25.00 cm^3 of sodium hydroxide solution, and she filled her burette with 2.0 mol/dm^3 sulphuric acid.

She did a rough trial, and then three accurate titrations. These are her results.

burette reading	trial	1	2	3
start	0.00	13.00	25.60	0.00
end	13.00	25.60	38.10	12.40
volume used in cm^3	13.00	12.60		

a Kim did not use her 'trial' value for her calculations. Explain why.

b Use Kim's three accurate readings to calculate an average value for the volume of sulphuric acid used. Show your working.

c Work out the number of moles of sulphuric acid used in the titration.

d This is the equation for the reaction.

$$2NaOH + H_2SO_4 \rightarrow Na_2SO_4 + 2H_2O$$

How many moles of NaOH react with each mole of sulphuric acid?

e How many moles of sodium hydroxide were in the 25 cm^3 of sodium hydroxide solution?

f What was the concentration of sodium hydroxide in Kim's titration? (Give your answer in moles per dm^3).

A6.1 Electrolysis reactions

Key points

- During electrolysis metals are discharged at the negative electrode and non-metals at the positive electrode.

- Electrolysis of ionic compounds when molten and when dissolved in water may produce different products.

1 Fill in the missing words using words from the list. Words may be used once, more than once or not at all.

> atoms carbon electrons gain ions
> lose metal molten negative positive
> protons solid solution

During electrolysis, metal or hydrogen _____ can be discharged at the _____ electrode. The metal _____ gain _____ from the negative electrode and become _____ Non-metal ions can be discharged at the _____ electrode. The non-metal ions _____ electrons. Sometimes, if the positive electrode is made from _____ , the metal _____ can lose _____ and dissolve into the electrolyte as metal _____ Electrolysis can only take place if the electrolyte is a _____ substance or an aqueous _____ .

2 Design a poster to explain how a metal wire conducts electricity. Include a labelled diagram and the words **metal ions** and **delocalised electrons**.

3 In each of the following statements about electrolysis **there is a mistake**. Rewrite the statements correctly by changing or removing **one** word each time.

a During electrolysis, if hydrogen is discharged it comes off as bubbles of gas at the positive electrode.

b The following elements all conduct electricity.

> **carbon copper iron sodium sulphur**

c When solid zinc chloride is electrolysed, zinc is discharged at the negative electrode and chlorine at the positive electrode.

d Molten salts can conduct electricity because their electrons are free to move.

e When a solution of aqueous copper(II) sulphate is electrolysed using copper electrodes, the positive electrode dissolves to give copper atoms in the water.

f Compounds which are liquid or in solution and which can undergo electrolysis contain covalent bonds.

g Molten aluminium oxide produces aluminium at the negative electrode and chlorine at the positive electrode.

4 The following substances are all electrolytes. Remember that (aq) means a solution in water, and (l) means molten or liquid. Write down the formulae of all the ions present. The first one has been done for you.

electrolyte	positive ions	negative ions
$NaCl(aq)$	Na^+ H^+	Cl^- OH^-
$HCl(aq)$		
$PbBr_2(l)$		
$CuSO_4(aq)$		
$NaOH(aq)$		
$KI(aq)$		
$ZnCl_2(l)$		
$NaBr(l)$		
$Ca(OH)_2(aq)$		
$(NH_4)_2SO_4(aq)$		
$Al_2O_3(l)$		
$NaNO_3(aq)$		

5 Write ionic equations to show how the following ions are discharged. The first one has been done for you.

a $H^+ + e^- \rightarrow H$

b $Cu^{2+} \rightarrow$

c $Cl^- \rightarrow$

d $OH^- \rightarrow$

e $Al^{3+} \rightarrow$

f $S^{2-} \rightarrow$

A6.2 Acidified water

Key points

- The electrolysis of dilute sulphuric acid produces hydrogen and oxygen gases.

- The quantity of electricity used in electrolysis can be related to the mass or volume of substance discharged.

1 Dilute sulphuric acid can be electrolysed using the apparatus in the diagram. The electrodes are made from carbon and any gases given off are collected in the test-tubes.

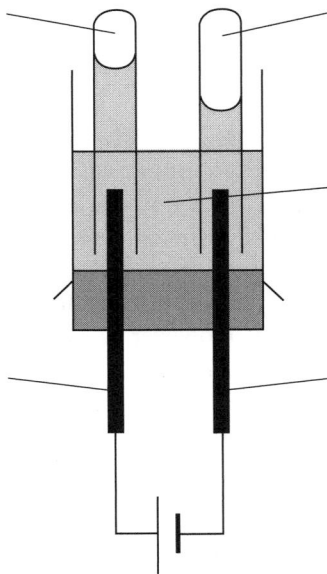

a Copy the diagram and label on it:
- the electrolyte, dilute sulphuric acid
- the negative electrode
- the name of the gas collected over the negative electrode
- the positive electrode
- the name of the gas collected over the positive electrode.

b What does this experiment indicate about the solubility of these gases in water?

c i Write down the symbols for the ions present in dilute sulphuric acid, $H_2SO_4(aq)$.
   ii Write down the symbols of the ions present in dilute sodium hydroxide, $NaOH(aq)$.
   iii What would you expect to happen when dilute sodium hydroxide is electrolysed?

2 State which products are formed at each electrode when the following compounds are electrolysed under the given conditions.

a molten anhydrous zinc chloride

b concentrated sodium chloride

c aqueous copper(II) sulphate using copper electrodes

3 Here are some ionic equations for the reactions which might occur when water containing a little sulphuric acid is electrolysed, using carbon electrodes. Only **one** from each set is correct. Identify the correct equation in each set.

a At the negative electrode:
   i $C \rightarrow C^{4+} - 4e^-$
   ii $H \rightarrow H^+ + e^-$
   iii $2H^+ + 2e^- \rightarrow H_2$

b At the positive electrode:
   i $SO_4^{2-} \rightarrow SO_4 + 2e^-$
   ii $4OH^- \rightarrow 2H_2O + O_2 + 4e^-$
   iii $H_2O \rightarrow 2H^+ + O^{2-}$

4

a What volume of hydrogen is released when a current of 4.0 A passes through an electrolysis cell containing dilute sulphuric acid for 48 minutes?

b What volume of oxygen is released under these conditions?

   Data: One mole of any gas at RTP occupies $24\,dm^3$.
   One Faraday of charge = 96 000 coulombs of electricity.

73

A6.3 Electrolysis in industry

Key points

- The electrolysis of brine produces hydrogen, chlorine and sodium hydroxide.

- Electrolysis can be used to coat a more reactive metal with a thin layer of a less reactive metal.

1 In the chlor-alkali industry, sodium chloride solution is electrolysed to make chlorine, hydrogen and sodium hydroxide. Here is a list of some of the important uses of the three products.

killing bacteria   making margarine
making soap   making ammonia
making rayon   making PVC plastic
making paper   making bleach
making CFCs   sterilising water
making sodium carbonate

Sort them out into a table to show the uses for each substance.

chlorine	hydrogen	sodium hydroxide

2 Design a poster to show the importance of sodium chloride as a raw material from which other substances are made. Use the information in question 1 to help you.

3 The diagram shows the design of a diaphragm cell. The porous membrane only allows sodium ions and water to pass through it.

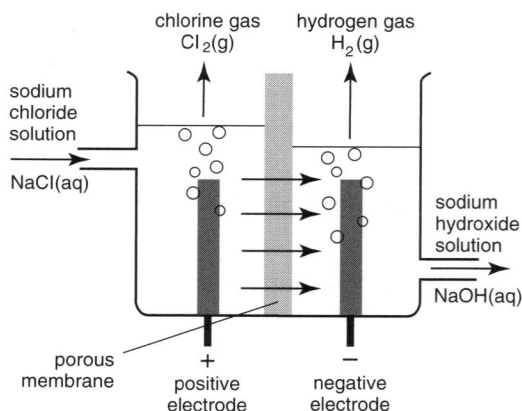

chlorine gas $Cl_2(g)$ hydrogen gas $H_2(g)$

sodium chloride solution
NaCl(aq)

sodium hydroxide solution
NaOH(aq)

porous membrane   positive electrode (+)   negative electrode (−)

a Aqueous sodium chloride flows into the positive electrode side of the cell. What are the ions present?

b Which ion is discharged at the positive electrode?

c Write an ionic equation to show what happens when the ion you have identified in **b** is discharged.

d What ions are present in the negative electrode side of the cell?

e Which ion is discharged at the negative electrode?

f Write an ionic equation to show how the ion you have identified in **e** is discharged.

g Why is it that the sodium hydroxide solution which flows out of the cell contains no chlorine?

h Why is it important to keep the hydrogen and chlorine gases separated?

i The first commercial cells for the electrolysis of sodium chloride solution used a negative electrode made from flowing mercury. Suggest why this caused environmental problems.

4 Steel can be protected from rusting by a layer of chromium plate. However, chromium does not easily stick to the steel so the steel is firstly electroplated with nickel, before the chromium plating process happens.

a Suggest how the steel can be electroplated with nickel.

b Suggest how the nickel plated steel can be electroplated with chromium.

5 80% of metallic zinc is produced by electrolysis.

a Zinc sulphide, ZnS, is firstly roasted in air to produce zinc oxide, ZnO, and sulphur dioxide, SO_2. Write an equation for this reaction.

b The sulphur dioxide can be converted into sulphuric acid by treatment with oxygen and water in the contact process. Zinc oxide is dissolved in this acid to produce zinc sulphate solution. This solution is electrolysed using negative electrodes made of aluminium on which zinc is discharged and eventually stripped off. Write an ionic equation to show how zinc ions are discharged.

c The positive electrodes are made from lead, at which oxygen gas is given off by discharge of hydroxide, OH⁻, ions. Copy and balance this ionic equation.

$$4OH^- \rightarrow H_2O + O_2 + 4e^-$$

d By considering the by-products made, explain why this process is an economic one.

Glossary (TB 1–8)

Terms in **_bold italic_** type are higher tier material.

A

abundant (2.3) – existing in large quantities.

acid (1.5) – substance that dissolves in water to form a solution with a pH below 7. An acid contains hydrogen which can replaced by a metal to form a salt.

addition polymer (6.5) – product formed when many molecules of a monomer react to form one large molecule. No other substances are formed.

addition reaction (6.3) – reaction in which two molecules react together to form one molecule.

alchemists (1.1) – alchemy combined aspects of chemistry with mysticism. It was developed in Egypt and China over 2000 years ago. In Europe the main aim of alchemists was to turn metals such as lead into gold.

algal bloom (8.4) – excessive growth of algae, e.g. during eutrophication.

alkali (1.5) – a metal oxide (called a base) or hydroxide that dissolves in water to form a solution with a pH above 7. An alkali is neutralised by an acid to form a salt and water.

alkane (6.3) – a family of hydrocarbons containing only single carbon to carbon bonds. Alkanes have a general formula C_nH_{2n+2}.

alkene (6.3) – family of hydrocarbons containing a carbon to carbon double bond. Alkenes have a general formula C_nH_{2n}.

alloy (2.5) – mixture of two or more metals, e.g. copper and zinc in brass.

anaerobic respiration (4.4) – respiration in the absence of oxygen. In yeast glucose reacts to form ethanol and carbon dioxide; in muscle lactic acid is formed.

atmospheres (8.1) – measurement of pressure. One atmosphere is approximately 100 000 Pa (100 000 N/m^2).

atomic number (3.1) – the number of protons in an atom of an element.

average bond energy (5.8) – the amount of energy required to break a typical type of covalent bond when more than one is present in a molecule, e.g. the average bond energy of a C—H bond in CH_4 is 413 kJ.

B

balanced equation (1.3) – a chemical equation where the number of each type of atom in the products is the same as the number of each type of atom in the reactants.

base (1.5) – a metal oxide which reacts with an acid to form a salt and water only.

bauxite (2.3) – the main ore of aluminium. It contains aluminium oxide, Al_2O_3.

biodegradable (6.6) – substances that can be broken down by such processes as decomposition by bacteria and can therefore be reused by living organisms.

bleach (3.7) – a solution containing chloride ions (Cl^-) and chlorate(I) ions (ClO^-) made by dissolving chlorine in sodium hydroxide solution. Bleach will decolourise dyes by oxidising them.

bond energy (5.8) – the amount of energy required to break a particular type of covalent bond. It is the same as the energy released when that bond forms.

brine (3.8) – a concentrated solution of sodium chloride in water.

buckminsterfullerene (5.6) – one form of the element carbon. It exists in the form of molecules, such as C_{60}, which has the same sort of a shape as a geodesic dome.

C

carcinogenic (6.1, 8.4) – causing cancer. Chemical carcinogens include tar and some dyes.

cast iron (2.2) – iron made by pouring the molten metal from the blast furnace into a mould and letting it cool.

catalyst (2.5, 4.3) – a substance which increases the rate of a chemical reaction but is itself unchanged in amount.

catalytic cracking (6.4) – breaking down of long-chain hydrocarbon molecules by the action of a heated catalyst to produce smaller molecules.

cement (1.4) – substance made by heating powdered limestone with clay. On mixing with water it sets to a hard mass.

chalk (1.4) – sedimentary rock consisting of very small particles of calcium carbonate.

chemical bonds (1.2) – name that is given to the forces that hold atoms together.

chemistry (1.1) – science of the elements and the ways in which they interact with each other.

collide (4.2) – make violent contact with another object.

colourless (3.9) – without colour.

combining power (1.2) – measure of the ability of an ion to combine with others. Magnesium has a combining power of two and chloride one. Two chloride ions join with one magnesium ion.

combustion (1.6, 6.2) – combination of a substance with oxygen to release energy.

concentration (4.2) – the quantity of a solute dissolved in a stated volume of solvent.

contact metamorphism (7.5) – a type of metamorphism that occurs when a rock has been altered by the effects of high temperatures. This often occurs when igneous intrusions pass near bedding planes of rock.

corrode (2.5) – suffer chemical attack.

corrosive (1.1) – a corrosive substance may damage your eyes and skin. It is represented by a tube dropping a liquid onto a hand in the Hazchem code.

covalent bond (3.6, 5.4) – type of bonding involving the sharing of one or more pairs of electrons. The electrons are provided by the atoms that are combining.

cracking (6.4) – breaking down of long-chain hydrocarbon molecules by the action of a heated catalyst or by heat alone to produce smaller molecules.

cryolite (2.3) – the mineral sodium aluminium fluoride, Na_3AlF_6. It is used as a solvent in the extraction of aluminium.

D

decomposers (8.4) – micro-organisms and small animals which break down the complex molecules in dead organic matter.

decomposition (4.3) – breaking a large molecule into smaller molecules.

denatured (4.4) – when the structure of a protein molecule is permanently changed, e.g. by high temperature or extreme pH.

denitrifying bacteria (7.2) – soil bacteria that break down nitrates, releasing nitrogen gas into the air.

density (3.5) – mass per unit of volume, e.g. kg/m^3 or g/cm^3.

diamond (5.6) – one form of the element carbon. The carbon atoms are held together by strong covalent bonds in a giant structure.

diatomic (3.9) – an element which exists naturally as molecules containing two atoms.

disinfectants (3.7) – substances which kill bacteria.

displacement reaction (3.6) – a reaction where one atom takes the place of another, e.g. iron taking the place of copper in copper(II) sulphate solution.

displayed formula (6.3) – chemical formula that shows every atom and bond. It is sometimes called a graphical formula or full structural formula.

dot and cross diagrams (5.2) – drawings representing the electrons in a molecule. Dots and crosses are used to indicate the atom from which the electron has originated.

double bond (5.4) – covalent bond in which there are two shared pairs of electrons between atoms, e.g. oxygen and ethene.

E

electrode (2.3) – an electrical connection from the power supply to a conductor such as an electrolyte.

electrolysis (2.1, 2.3) – the decomposition of a compound by the passage of electricity.

electrons (3.1, 3.10) – negatively charged sub-atomic particles which exist outside the nucleus.

electroplating (2.4) – covering one metal with a thin layer of another by the process of electrolysis.

electrostatic attraction (5.3) – attraction between opposite charges. Present in ionic compounds.

energy level diagram (5.8) – diagram showing the energy content at stages during a reaction.

endothermic (1.7, 2.2) – a reaction which takes in heat from the surroundings.

erosion (7.5) – process in which rocks are worn away.

eutrophication (8.4) – the process by which excessive quantities of nitrate ions pollute lakes and rivers.

exothermic (1.7) – reaction which gives out heat to the surroundings.

extrusive rocks (7.5) – igneous rocks that have cooled and solidified as crystals on the surface of the Earth, e.g. basalt.

F

fault (7.6) – beds of rocks that are distorted with a loss of continuity.

formula (1.2) – a chemical formula shows how many atoms of each element combine together to make a substance.

fossil (7.6) – recognisable remains of plants or animals that lived in the past.

fractional distillation (6.1) – method of separating liquids with different boiling points.

fold (7.6) – beds of rock that are distorted without loss of continuity.

G

gauze (8.2) – a mesh of fine wire.

giant structure (5.3) – a crystal structure in which all of the particles are linked together by a network of bonds extending through the crystal, e.g. diamond and sodium chloride.

glass (1.4) – supercooled liquid which forms a hard, brittle substance which is usually transparent. Common glass is made from limestone, sodium carbonate and sand.

global warming (7.4) – rise in the average temperature of the Earth's surface. It is thought to be caused by the greenhouse effect.

graphite (5.6) – one form of the element carbon. The carbon atoms are present in layers. These layers are only weakly held to each other.

greenhouse effect (7.4) – caused by the increase in concentration of atmospheric carbon dioxide and leading to global warming.

greenhouse gases (7.4) – gases such as carbon dioxide and methane that contribute to the greenhouse effect.

groups (3.2, 3.3) – vertical columns in the Periodic Table.

H

halide (3.8) – a compound containing the ions of a halogen (any element in Group 7).

harmful (1.1) – a harmful substance is poisonous but less so than a toxic substance. It is represented by a cross in the Hazchem code.

Hazchem code (1.1) – set of simple representations used to warn about the dangers from chemicals.

highly flammable (1.1) – substance that catches fire easily. It is represented by a flame in the Hazchem code.

hydrocarbon (6.1) – compounds made up from the elements carbon and hydrogen only.

I

igneous (7.5) – rocks that have cooled and solidified as crystals from molten rock.

inhibitor (4.3) – substance which makes a reaction take place more slowly.

intensive farming (8.3) – techniques to enable more food to be produced from less land.

intrusive rocks (7.5) – igneous rocks that have cooled and solidified as crystals inside the Earth, e.g. granite.

ion (3.1, 5.1) – positively or negatively charged particle formed when an atom or a group of atoms loses or gains electrons.

ionic bond (5.3) – type of bonding involving the complete transfer of one or more electrons from a metal atom to a non-metal atom. Ions are formed.

ionic compound (5.2) – compound formed by the electrostatic attraction between positive ions and negative ions.

ionic equation (1.3, 5.3) – concise method of writing down the important changes to ions in a chemical reaction. Ions that take no part in the reaction are not usually included.

isotopes (3.1, 3.10) – atoms of the same element but with different numbers of neutrons. They have the same atomic number but a different mass number.

K

khemeia (1.1) – the root of the word chemistry. Its origin was from ancient Egypt and described the secret processes that were used for embalming the dead.

L

laser (3.9) – an instrument used to produce an intense beam of light.

lava (7.5) – molten rock that escapes from a volcano.

lattice (5.3) – ionic bonding leads to the formation of a crystalline structure called a lattice.

leach (4.3, 8.4) – become washed out of soil or rock by the flow of water.

limekiln (1.4) – building in which limestone is roasted and turned into quicklime.

limestone (1.4) – rock made of calcium carbonate, $CaCO_3$.

liquefy (8.1) – turn from solid or gas into liquid.

M

magma (7.5) – rock between the crust and the core of the Earth.

manure (8.2, 8.3) – fertiliser made from animal faeces.

mass number (3.1) – sum of the number of protons and neutrons in an atom.

metamorphic rocks (7.5) – rocks that were originally either igneous or sedimentary and have been altered by the effects of high temperatures and/or high pressures.

micro-organism (4.4) – plant or animal which can only be seen by the use of a microscope.

minerals (2.1) – compounds contained within rocks.

molecular structure (5.5) – type of structure built up of molecules. A substance with a molecular structure has weak forces between molecules and so has a low melting point and boiling point.

molecule (1.3) – particle with two or more atoms joined together.

monatomic (3.9) – used to describe an element which exists naturally as individual atoms.

monomer (6.5) – small molecule which joins together with other molecules to produce a polymer.

N

neutralisation (1.5) – reaction in which an acid reacts with a base or alkali.

neutralising (8.2, 8.3) – cancelling out acidity or alkalinity to make the solution neutral.

neutrons (3.1, 3.10) – neutral sub-atomic particles which exist inside the nucleus.

nitrifying bacteria (7.2) – group of soil bacteria which convert ammonia to nitrates.

nitrogenous (8.4) – containing the element nitrogen.

non-metal (3.6) – an element which is not a metal.

nucleus (3.1, 3.10) – the central part of an atom. It contains protons and neutrons.

O

open-cast mining (2.3) – a technique that collects an ore from the surface of the Earth's crust.

optimum temperature (4.4) – the temperature at which maximum reaction takes place; used to describe the action of an enzyme.

optimum pH (4.4) – the pH at which maximum reaction takes place; used to describe the action of an enzyme.

ore (2.1) – a rock which contains a large percentage of a metal or metal compound.

oxidation (1.6) – reaction in which a substance gains oxygen or loses electrons. It is the opposite of reduction.

oxidise (6.2) – to bring about an oxidation process.

P

Periodic Table (1.2) – classification of the elements in order of their atomic numbers. Elements with similar properties appear in columns known as groups.

periods (3.3) – the horizontal rows of elements in the Periodic Table.

photosynthesis (7.2) – process taking place in the green parts of a plant. Water and carbon dioxide react together in sunlight and in the presence of chlorophyll to produce sugars and oxygen.

phytoplankton (7.3) – plankton consisting of plants.

pig iron (2.2) – impure iron produced by the blast furnace. It contains a high percentage of carbon.

plate tectonics (7.6) – slow movements of parts of the Earth's crust known as plates. The driving force for this movement is thought to be convection currents in the mantle.

pollutants (7.1) – contaminants of the environment that are a by-product of human activity.

polymer (6.5) – long chain molecule built up of a large number of small units, called monomers, joined together by a process called polymerisation.

precipitation (7.3) – the separation of a solid from a solution. The solid usually settles out.

pressure (4.2) – the force exerted on an object by the collision of particles of gas with the surface of the object.

products (1.3, 4.1) – the substances which remain after a chemical reaction has taken place. They appear to the right of the arrow in the equation.

properties (3.2) – what a chemical substance is like or what reactions it will undergo.

proteins (4.4, 8.3) – large molecules which are polymers of amino acids.

protons (3.1, 3.10) – positively charged sub-atomic particles which exist inside the nucleus.

Q

quicklime (1.4) – common name for calcium oxide, CaO.

R

rate of reaction (4.1) – the speed with which products are formed and reactants disappear during a chemical reaction.

reactants (1.3, 4.1) – substances that are used at the start of a chemical reaction. They appear to the left of the arrow in the equation.

reactivity (3.5) – how vigorously a substance reacts with other substances.

recycled (2.1) – used again.

redox reaction (2.4) – a reaction involving both reduction and oxidation.

reduction (1.6, 2.1) – reaction in which a substance loses oxygen or gains electrons. It is the opposite of oxidation.

relative atomic mass (3.10) – the mass of an atom measured on a scale where one atom of the isotope carbon-12 is exactly 12 units.

relative formula mass (5.7) – mass obtained by adding together the relative atomic masses of all of the atoms shown in the formula of a compound.

repeat unit (6.5) – that part of the structure of a polymer that repeats itself along the polymer chain.

rock salt (3.8) – impure salt (sodium chloride) which is present as deposits in the ground.

S

saturated (6.3) – compound which contains only single covalent bonds, e.g. ethane C_2H_6.

sedimentary rocks (7.5) – rocks, e.g. limestone and sandstone, that are composed of compacted fragments of older rocks that have accumulated in layers on the floor of an ancient sea or lake.

shells (3.4) – locations of electrons around the nucleus of an atom.

slag (2.2) – calcium silicate produced as a by-product of the blast furnace.

slaked lime (1.4) – common name for calcium hydroxide, $Ca(OH)_2$.

specific temperature (4.4) – a precise temperature.

stable (3.5) – not likely to take part in a chemical reaction.

state symbols (2.4) – symbols used in a chemical equation to indicate whether each substance is a solid (s), liquid (l), gas (g) or in solution in water (aq).

steel (2.2) – an alloy of iron with a small percentage (under 4%) of carbon.

sterilise (3.7) – kill bacteria.

succession (7.6) – layers of rock one above the other. Older rocks are usually at the bottom of the succession.

surface area (4.2) – the area of the surface of a solid object, usually measured in cm^2.

symbol (1.2) – one or two letters used to represent a chemical element. The first letter is always a capital.

symbol equation (1.3) – summary of a chemical reaction using the chemical symbols and formulae of the reactants and products.

T

thermal cracking (6.4) – breaking down of long-chain hydrocarbon molecules by the action of heat alone to produce smaller molecules.

thermal decomposition (1.4) – breaking down of compounds by the action of heat.

toxic (1.1) – poisonous substance. It is represented by a skull and crossbones in the Hazchem code. It is important not to swallow such substances or to get them on your skin.

U

unsaturated (6.3) – compound which contains at least one double bond, e.g. ethene C_2H_4.

W

weathering (7.5) – action of wind, rain, snow etc. on rocks. The action can be physical or chemical.

word equation (1.3) – summary of a chemical reaction using the chemical names of the reactants and products.

Y

yield (8.1) – the percentage of the maximum possible amount of a product which is actually produced in a chemical reaction.

Glossary (TB A1–A6)

Terms in **bold italic** type are higher tier material.

A

alcohol (A4.1) – an organic compound cotaining an OH group. A common alcohol is ethanol C_2H_5OH.

anhydrous (A6.1) – without water, e.g. anhydrous copper(II) sulphate.

aqueous (A6.1) – dissolved in water.

Avogadro constant (A5.1) – the number of particles in one mole of a sustance, 6×10^{23}.

B

brass (A3.1) – an alloy containing copper and zinc.

burette (A5.2) – a glass tube with a calibrated scale and tap. It is used to measure amounts of solutions, e.g. in titration.

C

conductivity (A2.2) – in chemistry used to indicate the extent to which a solution conducts electricity.

coulomb (A6.2) – the unit of electric charge. One coulomb of charge flows when one ampere of current passes for one second.

D

dehydration (A4.3) – a reaction where water, or the elements of water (hydrogen and oxygen), are removed from a substance.

discharged (A6.1) – formed at the positive or negative electrode during electrolysis.

E

empirical formula (A5.1) – a formula for a compound that shows the simplest ratio of atoms present.

F

Faraday (A6.2) – the electric charge which discharges one atomic mass in grams of a monovalent ion during electrolysis. It is 96 000 Coulombs.

fermentation (A4.3) – the procss in which enzymes in yeast convert glucose into ethanol and carbon dioxide.

G

galvanizing (A3.2) – covering steel with a layer of zinc, to prevent rusting.

general formula (A4.1) – a formula for a particular homologous series that shows the ratio of atoms present in general terms, e.g. alkenes have the general formula C_nH_{2n}.

H

homologous series (A4.1) – a family of organic compounds that have a general formula, e.g. the alkenes.

hydrated iron oxide (A3.2) – a form of iron(III) oxide combined with water molecules. It is the substance of rust.

I

ionic half equation (A3.3) – an ionic equation which represents only one of the two changes, reduction or oxidation, which take place in a redox reaction.

L

lather (A1.3) – the bubbles formed when soap is shaken with water.

lime scale (A1.3) – a deposit of calcium carbonate which is formed when water with temporary hardness is boiled. Sometimes called 'fur' in for examples kettles.

M

mole (A5.1) – the measure of amount of substance in chemistry. One mole of a substance has a mass equal to its relative formula mass in grams. One mole of any type of particle always contains the same number of particles, 6×10^{23}.

molecular formula (A5.1) – a formula which shows the actual number of atoms present in a molecule.

O

organic chemistry (A4.1) – the chemistry of carbon containing compounds. There are many millions of organic compounds.

oxidizing agent (A3.3) – a substance which brings out the oxidation of another substance.

P

permanent hardness, of water (A1.2) – hardness of water which is not removed by boiling the water. It is caused by dissolved calcium and magnesium sulphates.

pH meter (A2.2) – a device that allows the pH of a solution to be found without the need for indicators.

pipette (A5.2) – a graduated glass tube for delivering a measured quantity of liquid or solution. Used in volumetric analysis.

R

redox reaction (A3.3) – a reaction involving both reduction and oxidation.

reducing agent (A3.3) – a substance which brings about the reduction of another substance.

S

sacrificial protection (A2) – the corrosion of a more reactive metal in contact with a less reactive metal, which stops the less reactive metal corroding, e.g. zinc in contact with iron prevents the iron from rusting.

saturated solution (A1.1) – a solution which contains the maximum mass of a solute that will dissolve in the solvent at that temperature.

scum (A1.3) – the solid formed when soap is mixed with hard water.

solder (A3.1) – an alloy containing tin and lead, used to make joins in electrical circuits.

solubility (A1.1) – the maximum mass of a solute which will dissolve in a given volume of solvent at a specified temperature.

solubility curve (A1.1) – a graph showing how the solubility of a solute in a solvent changes with change in temperature.

solute (A1.1) – the substance which dissolves in a solvent to make a solution.

solution (A1.1) – the liquid formed when a solute dissolves in a solvent, e.g. brine is a solution of salt (sodium chloride) as the solute in water as the solvent.

solvent (A1.1) – the liquid which dissolves a solute to make a solution.

spectator ions (A2.2) – ions that are present when a chemical reaction takes place but take no part in the reaction.

stainless steel (A3.2) – an alloy containing iron, chromium and nickel and a small proportion of carbon. It is resistant to corrosion.

strong acid (A2.1) – an acid that completely ionizes when it dissolves in water.

structural isomers (A4.2) – substances that have the same molecular formula but different structures.

T

temporary hardness, of water (A1.2) – hardness of water which is removed by boiling. It is caused by dissolved calcium or magnesium hydrogencarbonate.

titration (A5.2) – a method of investigating the volumes of solutions that react together.

W

water hardness (A1.2) – the difficulty in forming a lather in water caused by the presence of calcium and magnesium ions.

water softener (A1.2) – a method used to remove hardness from water.

weak acid (A2.2) – an acid that only partly ionozed when it dissolves in water and produces a low concentration of hydrogen ions, H^+.

The Periodic Table of the Elements

Group

1	2								Transition metals									3	4	5	6	7	0
								1 **H** Hydrogen 1															4 **He** Helium 2
7 **Li** Lithium 3	9 **Be** Beryllium 4																	11 **B** Boron 5	12 **C** Carbon 6	14 **N** Nitrogen 7	16 **O** Oxygen 8	19 **F** Fluorine 9	20 **Ne** Neon 10
23 **Na** Sodium 11	24 **Mg** Magnesium 12																	27 **Al** Aluminium 13	28 **Si** Silicon 14	31 **P** Phosphorus 15	32 **S** Sulphur 16	35.5 **Cl** Chlorine 17	40 **Ar** Argon 18
39 **K** Potassium 19	40 **Ca** Calcium 20	45 **Sc** Scandium 21	48 **Ti** Titanium 22	51 **V** Vanadium 23	52 **Cr** Chromium 24	55 **Mn** Manganese 25	56 **Fe** Iron 26	59 **Co** Cobalt 27	59 **Ni** Nickel 28	64 **Cu** Copper 29	65 **Zn** Zinc 30							70 **Ga** Gallium 31	73 **Ge** Germanium 32	75 **As** Arsenic 33	79 **Se** Selenium 34	80 **Br** Bromine 35	84 **Kr** Krypton 36
85 **Rb** Rubidium 37	88 **Sr** Strontium 38	89 **Y** Yttrium 39	91 **Zr** Zirconium 40	93 **Nb** Niobium 41	96 **Mo** Molybdenum 42	99 **Tc** Technetium 43	101 **Ru** Ruthenium 44	103 **Rh** Rhodium 45	106 **Pd** Palladium 46	108 **Ag** Silver 47	112 **Cd** Cadmium 48							115 **In** Indium 49	119 **Sn** Tin 50	122 **Sb** Antimony 51	128 **Te** Tellurium 52	127 **I** Iodine 53	131 **Xe** Xenon 54
133 **Cs** Caesium 55	137 **Ba** Barium 56	139 **La** Lanthanum 57 *	178 **Hf** Hafnium 72	181 **Ta** Tantalum 73	184 **W** Tungsten 74	186 **Re** Rhenium 75	190 **Os** Osmium 76	192 **Ir** Iridium 77	195 **Pt** Platinum 78	197 **Au** Gold 79	201 **Hg** Mercury 80							204 **Tl** Thallium 81	207 **Pb** Lead 82	209 **Bi** Bismuth 83	209 **Po** Polonium 84	210 **At** Astatine 85	222 **Rn** Radon 86
223 **Fr** Francium 87	226 **Ra** Radium 88	227 **Ac** Actinium 89 †																					

Lanthanides (*)

140 **Ce** Cerium 58	141 **Pr** Praseodymium 59	144 **Nd** Neodymium 60	147 **Pm** Promethium 61	150 **Sm** Samarium 62	152 **Eu** Europium 63	157 **Gd** Gadolinium 64	159 **Tb** Terbium 65	162 **Dy** Dysprosium 66	165 **Ho** Holmium 67	167 **Er** Erbium 68	169 **Tm** Thulium 69	173 **Yb** Ytterbium 70	175 **Lu** Lutetium 71

Actinides (†)

232 **Th** Thorium 90	231 **Pa** Protactinium 91	238 **U** Uranium 92	237 **Np** Neptunium 93	244 **Pu** Plutonium 94	243 **Am** Americium 95	247 **Cm** Curium 96	247 **Bk** Berkelium 97	251 **Cf** Californium 98	252 **Es** Einsteinium 99	257 **Fm** Fermium 100	258 **Md** Mendelevium 101	259 **No** Nobelium 102	260 **Lr** Lawrencium 103

Key

a = relative atomic mass
X = atomic symbol
b = proton (atomic) number

a
X
b

Key data

Relative atomic masses

This table gives the relative atomic mass of common elements, which you will need to refer when answering questions in this book.

name	symbol	relative atomic mass A_r
aluminium	Al	27
bromine	Br	80
calcium	Ca	40
carbon	C	12
chlorine	Cl	35.5
copper	Cu	64
fluorine	F	19
hydrogen	H	1
iodine	I	127
iron	Fe	56
lead	Pb	207
magnesium	Mg	24
nitrogen	N	14
oxygen	O	16
phosphorus	P	31
silver	Ag	108
sodium	Na	23
sulphur	S	32
zinc	Zn	65

The reactivity series of some metals

most reactive	
potassium	
sodium	
calcium	the non-metal
magnesium	carbon is between
aluminium	aluminium and zinc
zinc	
iron	
tin	the non-metal
lead	hydrogen is between
copper	lead and copper
silver	
gold	
least reactive	

Some examples of rock types

igneous	metamorphic	sedimentary
basalt	gneiss	chalk
dolerite	marble	limestone
gabbro	schist	mudstone
granite	slate	sandstone

Formulae of some common ions

Positive ions

name	formula
aluminium	Al^{3+}
ammonium	NH_4^+
barium	Ba^{2+}
calcium	Ca^{2+}
copper(II)	Cu^{2+}
hydrogen	H^+
iron(II)	Fe^{2+}
iron(III)	Fe^{3+}
lead	Pb^{2+}
lithium	Li^+
magnesium	Mg^{2+}
potassium	K^+
silver	Ag^+
sodium	Na^+
zinc	Zn^{2+}

Negative ions

name	formula
bromide	Br^-
carbonate	CO_3^{2-}
chloride	Cl^-
fluoride	F^-
hydrogencarbonate	HCO_3^-
hydroxide	OH^-
iodide	I^-
nitrate	NO_3^-
oxide	O^{2-}
sulphate	SO_4^{2-}

Data about elements

This table gives information about some of the elements.

atomic number	name of element	formula	structure	date of discovery	m.p. in °C	b.p. in °C
13	aluminium	Al	giant atomic	1827	659	2447
18	argon	Ar	single atoms	1894	−189	−186
33	arsenic	As		1250	613	(sublimes)
56	barium	Ba	giant atomic	1808	710	1637
4	beryllium	Be	giant atomic	1798	1283	2487
35	bromine	Br_2	molecules	1826	−7	58
55	caesium	Cs	giant atomic	1860	29	685
20	calcium	Ca	giant atomic	1808	850	1492
6	carbon	C	giant molecular	ancient	3550	4827
17	chlorine	Cl_2	molecules	1774	−101	−34
24	chromium	Cr	giant atomic	1797	1903	2642
27	cobalt	Co	giant atomic	1735	1495	2877
29	copper	Cu	giant atomic	ancient	1083	2582
9	fluorine	F_2	molecules	1887	−220	−188
79	gold	Au	giant atomic	ancient	1063	2707
2	helium	He	single atoms	1868	−270	−269
1	hydrogen	H_2	molecules	1766	−259	−253
53	iodine	I_2	molecules	1811	114	184
26	iron	Fe	giant atomic	ancient	1539	2887
36	krypton	Kr	single atoms	1898	−157	−153
82	lead	Pb	giant atomic	ancient	328	1751
3	lithium	Li	giant atomic	1818	181	1331
12	magnesium	Mg	giant atomic	1808	650	1117
25	manganese	Mn	giant atomic	1774	1244	2041
80	mercury	Hg		ancient	−39	357
10	neon	Ne	single atoms	1898	−248	−246
28	nickel	Ni	giant atomic	1751	1455	2837
7	nitrogen	N_2	molecules	1772	−210	−196
8	oxygen	O_2	molecules	1774	−219	−183
15	phosphorus	P_4	molecules	1669	44	281
78	platinum	Pt	giant atomic	1735	1770	3827
19	potassium	K	giant atomic	1807	63	766
14	silicon	Si	giant molecular	1824	1410	2677
47	silver	Ag	giant atomic	ancient	961	2127
11	sodium	Na	giant atomic	1807	98	890
16	sulphur	S_8	molecules	ancient	119	445
50	tin	Sn	giant atomic	ancient	232	2687
30	zinc	Zn	giant atomic	1746	419	908

Electron arrangement

Electron arrangements for the first 20 elements

element	1st shell	2nd shell	3rd shell	4th shell
hydrogen	1			
helium	2			
lithium	2	1		
beryllium	2	2		
boron	2	3		
carbon	2	4		
nitrogen	2	5		
oxygen	2	6		
fluorine	2	7		
neon	2	8		
sodium	2	8	1	
magnesium	2	8	2	
aluminium	2	8	3	
silicon	2	8	4	
phosphorus	2	8	5	
sulphur	2	8	6	
chlorine	2	8	7	
argon	2	8	8	
potassium	2	8	8	1
calcium	2	8	8	2

Index